Marriage Enrichment

Executive Producer: *Richard A. Weimer*
Cover and Text Design: *Marlise Reidenbach*
Art Director: *Don Sellers*
Illustrations: *Mary Angle*

MARRIAGE ENRICHMENT
Philosophy, Process, and Program

Larry Hof, M. Div. and
William R. Miller, Ph.D.

Robert J. Brady Co.
A Prentice-Hall Publishing and
Communications Company
Bowie, Maryland 20715

Marriage enrichment

Library of Congress Cataloging in Publication Data

Hof, Larry.
    Marriage enrichment.
      1. Marriage counseling—United States.
2. Family—United States.   3. Interpersonal
relations.   I. Miller, William Ross, 1947–
joint author.   II. Title.
HQ10. H59   306.8   80–11081

ISBN 0–87619–717–9

Prentice-Hall International, Inc., London
Prentice-Hall of Australia, Pty., Ltd., Sydney
Prentice-Hall of India Private Limited, New Delhi
Prentice-Hall of Japan, Inc., Tokyo
Prentice-Hall of Southeast Asia Pte. Ltd., Singapore
Whitehall Books, Limited, Petone, New Zealand

Printed in the United States of America

81 82 83 84 85 86 87 88 89 90   10 9 8 7 6 5 4 3 2 1

With love and appreciation, we dedicate
this book to Millie and Beth.

Contents

Foreword

The marriage enrichment (ME) movement, a product of the decade of the 1970s, is growing rapidly, gaining momentum, and will become in my estimation an important social force in the next decade. The social upheavals of the 1960s with its violent, often intergenerational, conflicts in values, were succeeded by a period of increasing disappointment in the ability of elected officials to govern effectively. Ineffective governing, a national moral vacuum, and the threat of economic collapse have created a situation in which married people increasingly turn toward each other for emotional support. Unfortunately, all too often, marital partners are frustrated and baffled by their seeming inability to give or get what they are seeking from each other. Given a reasonable fit between them, somehow they learn that there are a set of skills and a whole body of knowledge about marriage that can greatly improve their capacity to meet each other's emotional needs. This is the rationale for ME, a movement designed to meet the requests of hundreds of thousands of couples for additional knowledge and skills for their most important adult relationship.

In the middle class, at least during this century, when actual physical survival was not its major preoccupation, marriage and the family has had the paradoxically dual capacity of providing a haven from the battering of economic and social storms, and of itself becoming a major stress, creating a crack and possibly an irrevocable split in the family fabric.

Most people seem to enter marriage with two opposing sets of expectations, namely, that marriage will bring happiness, personal fulfillment, and emotional security, and a vague fear, given the knowledge that so many marriages break up or otherwise fail, that the relationship with the spouse will be a source of disillusionment and pain. When external forces such as government or other social institutions like the church fail to provide a sense of security, people turn to other movements often involving groups sharing similar needs, or they turn to each other. More and more, people are finding that they are unable to obtain emotional ease and security from vaguely transcendental programs such as TM or EST, or the encounter groups so prevalent in our society. With good common sense they are discovering that these ubiquitous needs can be satisfied at home more effectively and at less cost financially and emotionally. If the marital unit is strengthened, that is, enriched, the entire family is apt to benefit and the family does indeed become a protective canopy under which each member has a greater opportunity to develop his or her own potential.

In the early phases of creating new ways of helping people develop new skills, many different methods are tried, a form of trial-and-error, until the more appropriate ways are selected and retained. When the skills to be learned are interpersonal, multiple approaches are essential because we are far less certain about what constitutes effective teaching and learning in the area of human relations than we are in learning how to drive a car, to type, learn a new language, or become a computer-programmer. Marriage enrichment, no exception to the rule, has provided many different methods. That is all to the good, for only in this way can the ineffective ways be discarded, with a firmer conviction that one is on a more solid footing in advocating the more salutory approaches.

It is now appropriate, however, to make a detailed examination of the various methods of ME, to find their commonalities as well as differences, to attempt to see if their objectives are reasonable and attainable, given the teaching techniques used, if there is new learning of interpersonal marital skills, and if these are maintained over a reasonable time. In this volume, Hof and Miller have met the readers' expectations in that they describe in detail a new field, compare different approaches, and suggest additional research to overcome the gaps in knowledge. The first half of the book describes the state of the art of marriage enrichment, and the second half develops in great detail the ME program now in use at the Marriage Council of Philadelphia. The second half, then, is a how-to-do-it book in itself, a great aid to new students in the field who wish to gain the knowledge and skills of an ME trainer; those already familiar with ME can compare teaching objectives, methods, format, and techniques.

If the ME field can be compared to a baby, research in ME is a week-old infant. To me, the chapter on research is the most valuable one in the book, for it indicates the areas where additional information is needed. Outcome studies are vital if we are to understand how these marital and personal skills are put to use by couples long after the ME program has ended. To be successful, ME programs must model the process of communication and emotional exchange based on mutual trust and respect, so that over time, these become automatic and ingrained and are used rather effortlessly and not in an awkward, artificial, or stilted manner.

We also need to know whether the ME programs are as suitable for blue-collar workers as they are for the middle class. Will they work just as well in black as in white marriages? What difference does it make if the participants are patients in couple-therapy, or are people who have never received couple-counseling? Can we refine our understanding of the process of marriage enrichment so that we can sort out the variance among the three primary factors, namely a supportive environment, behavioral modification, and the effects of participating in a group? As a marital therapist, I would be most interested in knowing to what extent these programs enhance, speed up, or possibly interfere with the treatment I am conducting with individual couples. While ME is primarily an educational technique, does it also have an important use as adjuvant therapy for those with troubled marriages?

The potential for the growth of ME programs is enormous. It is clear that in their individual adaptation people need the help they cannot get from society at large or from the group movements that have sprung up. If marital skills can be developed to the point where marriage greatly enhances our feelings of "integrity and generativity," to use Eric Erikson's terms, it will decrease the percentage of failed marriages which, in turn, are a potent source of mental and physical illness.

We live in a society in which the pace of technological progress increases at an exponential rate. At the same time, our emotional lives have not evolved very far from those of the caveman. For society to survive, there has to be a leap forward in emotional development that parallels the breathtaking technological achievements the world has witnessed in the last century. Any program that enhances our capacity to significantly develop more satisfying marital relationships may be one of the most important responses society can make to bridge the enormous distance between technology and emotion.

Harold I. Lief, M.D.
Professor of Psychiatry
Director, Division of Family Study,
University of Pennsylvania
Director, Marriage Council of
Philadelphia

Preface

The approaches to marriage enrichment are analogous to, but more varied than, the colors of the rainbow. From a distance, each approach or color appears to be a totally distinct and unique entity. Upon closer examination, however, we realize that the various programs or colors flow from and merge with each other. Instead of being completely separate entities, each is seen to be directly related to those on either side of it, and to share certain important aspects with each other.

Scientists thoroughly understand the relationship of the colors of the rainbow to each other. Scientific theory and spectrographic analysis have provided the base for that understanding, an understanding which can be conveyed in such simple terms that a small child can grasp it, or in such complex forms that advanced training is needed to comphrehend the concepts being expressed. We cannot say the same with regard to the new field of marriage enrichment, because, to date, few attempts have been made to link the many approaches and programs together.

For the last few years, we have discussed informally what we believe to be the underlying philosophy and theoretical foundation of most marriage enrichment programs and the common elements of the process of marriage enrichment. One of our main purposes in writing this book is to present, in a more formal way, an integrated overview of the philosophy, process, programs, and target populations of marriage enrichment, as well as a critical review of the current research on such programming. Becuase this first section of the book represents a summary of the available literature, it is highly documented with references. We hope this effort will help to synthesize the information and establish some degree of order to the expanding literature and research on marriage enrichment.

Our second purpose, in Section II of the book, is to present a comprehensive description of our own Creative Marriage Enrichment Program used at the Marriage Council of Philadelphia. We hope this presentation will allow readers to get a sense of what one approach to marriage enrichment is like. The discussion of the theoretical foundation of the program, the specific goals and objectives, and the detailed description of the actual procedures and exercises employed, make it possible for the clinician, educator, clergy-person, or appropriately trained lay person to use the book as a program manual for conducting marriage enrichment programs based upon this model.

We do not view marriage enrichment programs as a substitute for marital therapy, when that is indicated. Nor, do we view participation in such programs as the panacea which will save the institution of marriage in our society. What we do believe, however, is that couples who have adopted the philosophy of marriage enrichment, who are involved in the ongoing process of marriage enrichment, and who participate in marriage enrichment programs that meet their specific needs, will be better able to maximize their potential as individuals and as a married couple, and to cope with the stresses and problems that emerge when two people live together in an intimate relationship. We also believe that marital therapy may be enhanced by marriage enrichment programming. Granted, we must await further research to make these statements in a more definitive way. For now, we are content to offer this book as a step in what we believe to be the right direction.

Larry Hof, M. Div.
William R. Miller, Ph.D.

Acknowledgments

We would like to express our appreciation to our friends at Saint Andrew's United Methodist Church, who helped give birth to the Creative Marriage Enrichment Program. Without their willing participation and constructive suggestions, the program would not have reached its present form. We also appreciate the help of Dave and Janice Cramp, and Blair and Sandy Monie, who offered many helpful suggestions as they led several pilot programs.

We would like to thank our colleagues at the Marriage Council of Philadelphia, who offered continued support and encouragement. We appreciate the help of our secretaries, Jean McLaughlin and Shirley Jacoby, for their typing skills and patience with us as we continually revised the manuscript.

The senior author would like to express special appreciation to Arnold Nakajima and Cecil Benoit who, as teachers, mentors, and friends, encouraged him to grow and write.

Lastly, we want to especially acknowledge our wives, Millie Hof and Beth Miller, and our children, Carolyn and David Hof and Will and Sarah Miller. Throughout the preparation of this manuscript, they helped us to pass through some discouraging and grouchy times, as they continued to give us their joy, love, patience and support.

SECTION I

Marriage Enrichment: An Overview

In this section of the book we will present an overview of the literature on marriage enrichment, including discussions of the philosophy, the process, types of programs, leadership, target populations, and research. Because this is based on so many sources, the text here is heavily referenced.

The Philosophy of Marriage Enrichment

DEFINITION*

Marriage Enrichment is an educational and preventive approach to relationship enhancement. The term refers to the philosophy and process of this approach as well as to a great variety of programs. The aim of marriage enrichment is to assist couples in achieving the following goals: 1) to increase each person's self-awareness and the awareness of his or her partner, especially regarding the positive aspects, strengths, and growth potential of the individuals and the marriage; 2) to increase exploration and self-disclosure of the partners' thoughts and feelings; 3) to increase mutual empathy and intimacy; and 4) to develop and encourage the use of skills needed by the partners for effective communication, problem solving and conflict resolution. The most popular programs are those designed for couples who want to improve an already well-functioning marriage (Otto, 1976). However, an increasing number of practitioners are offering marriage enrichment programs to couples identified as troubled, dysfunctional, or clinical.

The origin of the term marriage enrichment is unclear, but other terms such as marital enrichment, marital growth, and preventive marital

---

*This book focuses almost exclusively on marriage enrichment, and does not give equal consideration to family enrichment because of our belief that the most effective and efficient way to enrich families is to focus on the husband–wife relationship. We believe that the quality of that relationship greatly influences, and may in fact determine, the quality of the total family relationship. This does not negate the value of looking upon the family as an integrated system, but rather emphasizes the central importance of the subsystem of the marital dyad in the larger system of the family. We believe that marriage enrichment can result in a motivation for, and actualization of family enrichment; therefore, we have chosen to focus our energy in this direction.

health are frequently used as synonyms. Although there may be difficulty in establishing the origins of the term, there is little difficulty in identifying a reason for the emergence of marriage enrichment programs when one considers the question, "What does the future hold for the institution of marriage?" There are many indications that suggest the outlook for marriage is not very bright. Rising divorce rates, the ever present reality of violence between marital partners and within families, and the apparent long-term dissatisfaction between marital partners who stay married do not augur well for the future.

One of the underlying problems appears to be that many people enter marriage expecting instant gratification and pleasure, and demanding their rights as individuals. Glasser and Glasser (1977) have expressed the concern of many that the emphasis on the values of individualism and hedonism in our society may be making a significant contribution to the difficulties facing marriage and the family, and to the disillusionment, conflict, and unhappiness which frequently prevail.

Additionally, the impact of the human potential and the women's liberation movements have contributed to the problem. Personal development or self-development has been increasingly emphasized in our society since the personal growth and small group movements burst into full bloom in the 1960s. The women's liberation movement has led an increasing number of women to be assertive, or at least more communicative, regarding their wants, needs, and aspirations. Words and phrases such as self-actualization, achieving personal potential, autonomy, open communication, gender equality, role flexibility, and intimacy, pervade the popular and professional literature. Such an emphasis has been needed to offset the values of self-denial and self-depreciation which seemed to characterize our society during much of the first half of this century. But, if the pendulum swings too far in the opposite direction, individualism and hedonism can run rampant.

A consequence of these movements has been a growing unwillingness on the part of many individuals to stay in an unsatisfactory marriage. The relaxing of legal and other external social barriers to divorce has made it relatively easy for such people to terminate relationships which are not emotionally satisfying.

Yet, the fact remains that despite the presence of so much dissatisfaction within marriage, and despite the presence of the availability of a variety of alternative life-styles, millions of people choose to marry each year. In addition to first marriages, a majority of those who divorce desire to marry again, and, in fact, do. The values of hedonism and individualism may doom many of these first and subsequent marriage relationships to failure, but the apparently pervasive "myth of naturalism" (Vincent, 1973, 1977) is even more insidious.

This myth expresses the belief that people who marry automatically know how to live and relate effectively together, and that they can continue to have effective interpersonal relationships without any concerted effort on their parts. It is often related to the myth that there is a standardized normal or good marriage, and the belief that couples do not have to create their own set of flexible, continually growing, and changing standards (Lederer and Jackson, 1968). Because of the myth of naturalism, people do not adequately prepare for marriage or see any real need for continuing education in effective interpersonal relating after marriage. They also fail to consider the possibility that a marriage, like any in-depth relationship, may stagnate or tend towards inertia unless it is revitalized continually by conscious choice and concerted action. It really is not surprising, then, that so much disenchantment and disillusionment with marriage exists when people are demanding so much from it and are giving so little preparation and ongoing effort to making it effective and mutually satisfying.

The marriage enrichment movement has emerged in response to these serious problems facing marriage today. Its proponents refuse to see the outlook for the future of marriage as dim. Instead, they affirm the possibility that people can develop (not find) personal fulfillment and interpersonal intimacy *within the marital relationship.* They have committed themselves to affirming and stabilizing marriage in our society by challenging and helping people to develop their marital relationship continually, mutually and reciprocally, in a disciplined, committed, and responsible way.

Since the early 1960s, when marriage enrichment programming began, it is estimated that well over a million couples have participated in the programs in the United States and Canada. Such numbers, if anywhere near accurate, indicate that the marriage enrichment movement is touching the lives of enormous numbers of people and is therefore deserving of careful examination.

HISTORICAL PERSPECTIVE

The marriage enrichment movement has emerged from a variety of sources. The Roman Catholic Marriage Encounter program began in Spain in January, 1962, under the initiative and leadership of Father Gabriel Calvo. It grew out of a desire to help families to relate more effectively together, and Father Calvo's belief that it was necessary to start with the relationship of the marital dyad (Demarest, Sexton and Sexton, 1977). The program reached the United States in 1967, and over 200,000 couples have participated (Genovese, 1975). Because of the strong links with the Roman Catholic Church, some perceived sense of exclusivism, and differing needs, several Protestant and Jewish versions of Marriage Encounter have developed.

David and Vera Mace began their work with retreats for the Quakers in October, 1962 (Mace and Mace, 1974b, 1978). Herbert Otto was conducting a variety of experimental programs in the area of marital and family enrichment as early as 1961 (Mace and Mace, 1978; Otto, 1969). Leon and Antoinette Smith were conducting programs in the mid 1960s, and they initiated the first leadership training program for couples in 1966 (Mace and Mace, 1978). Sherod Miller and his associates were conducting their studies in marital communication in the late 1960s, and they eventually developed the Minnesota Couples Communication Program (now known as the Couples Communication Program). Undoubtedly, many other people were doing concurrent exploratory work in the area of marriage enrichment and marital communication. The relative infancy of the movement is demonstrated by the fact that in a survey of 30 professionals conducted by Otto (1975, 1976), 90 percent conducted their first program in 1973 or later.

In 1973, the Association of Couples for Marriage Enrichment (ACME) was founded by David and Vera Mace. Under its auspices, the Council of Affiliated Marriage Enrichment Organizations (CAMEO) was formed in 1975, and has concerned itself primarily with developing leadership and training standards. The Association of Couples for Marriage Enrichment (ACME) was created with the following four-fold purpose: "1) to encourage and help member couples to seek growth and enrichment in their own marriages; 2) to organize activities through which member couples can help each other in their quest for marital growth and enrichment; 3) to promote and support effective community services designed to foster successful marriages; 4) to seek to improve the public image of marriage as a relationship capable of fostering both personal growth and mutual fulfillment" (Hopkins, Hopkins, Mace and Mace, 1978, p. 21).

ACME is made up of many different agencies, programs, and couples. Current membership (1979) is approximately 1800 lay and professional couples, with members in all 50 states, 6 Canadian provinces, and 13 other countries (Hopkins et al., 1978). There are over 50 local chapters in North America, and State, Regional, and North American Conferences on Marriage Enrichment have been held at various places in the United States under the auspices of ACME.

Marriage enrichment programs are not limited to the United States, but this country does appear to be the leader in the field at present (Otto, 1975). The human potential movement and the encounter and small group movement have clearly been the forerunners of the marriage enrichment movement in America, contributing greatly to the philosophy, process, and program design of most programs (Otto, 1976). The movement in America, since its inception, has also had strong roots in many religious or faith systems (Hopkins and Hopkins, 1975), becuase of their keen interest in the family and their concern for the future of marriage and the family. There are at least 14 marriage enrichment programs which are national in scope and directly connected to an established religious organization. However, there are many other programs which do not have religious affiliations, such as the Couples Communication Program, Family Service Association of America, Marriage Effectiveness Training, and the Relationship Enhancement Programs.

Many of the marriage enrichment programs which have been developed to date are local in scope, in that they have been developed and are used, for the most part, by a particular individual or couple and associates within a small geographical area. The Pairing Enrichment Program (Travis and Travis, 1975) and the Marriage Diagnostic Laboratory (MARDILAB) (Stein, 1975) are examples of such programs. Other programs are national in scope, in terms of organization, leadership training, and location. Some of the programs included in this category are, Marriage Encounter (Bosco, 1973; Demarest et al., 1977; Genovese, 1975), Marriage Communication Labs (Smith and Smith, 1976), Relationship Enhancement Programs (Guerney, 1977), Couples Communication Program (Miller, Nunnally, and Wackman, 1976a), the Association of Couples for Marriage Enrichment (ACME) (Hopkins et al., 1978), and the enrichment programs developed by L'Abate and Collaborators (1975).

There are at least fifty different programs known to the authors, some of which have been attended by as few as ten couples, and others that have been attended by thousands of couples (Mace, Note 1; Otto, 1976). In that group of fifty are included several educational therapy programs developed and conducted by marital therapists and counselors (e.g., Bolte, 1975; Smith and Alexander, 1974). In 1973 and 1974, Otto surveyed various marriage and family enrichment programs in the United States and Canada and concluded that at least 420,000 couples have been participants [over 3500 in the Couples Communication Program; over 7000 in the United Methodist Communication Labs; over 400,000 in the various expressions of Marriage Encounter, with almost 60,000 couples being added each year (Gallagher, 1975)]. Currently, he estimates that at least twice that number now have participated in enrichment programs, due to the increasing number of facilitators and programs which have come to his attention since his initial survey.

We will now take a closer look at the philosophical foundation of marriage enrichment and examine some of the common elements of this movement which has touched the lives of so many people.

GROWTH ORIENTATION

At the core of marriage enrichment is a positive, growth-oriented, and potential-oriented philosophy of the individual. In her book, *Our Inner Con-*

flicts, Karen Horney expresses this optimistic view of human nature and the potential in people for growth, development, and change. She writes, "My own belief is that man has the capacity as well as the desire to develop his potentialities and become a decent human being, and that these deteriorate if this relationship to others and hence to himself is, and continues to be, disturbed. I believe that man can change and go on changing as long as he lives. And this belief has grown with deeper understanding" (Horney, 1945, p. 19). Proponents of marriage enrichment frequently verbalize this positive aspect to program participants, encouraging them to see change as possible and to accept continuing responsibility for the growth and development of their personal and interpersonal life.

Thus, the keystone of marriage enrichment is growth and human potential, based on the premise that all persons and relationships have a great many untapped strengths and resources which can be developed (Mace and Mace, 1975, 1976a; Otto, 1976). People are viewed as having a natural drive towards growth, health, and personal development. Given the appropriate environment people can learn how to choose and change behaviors and attitudes which will improve their interpersonal relationships, and allow them to experience increased satisfaction in life and in relationships with other people. Problems and conflicts are not ignored, but are faced with the affirmation that people can learn how to cope with them in a creative and positive way and develop a more fulfilling life.

DYNAMIC VIEW OF MARRIAGE

The proponents of marriage enrichment view marriage in the same positive and growth-oriented light. It is affirmed that the marriage relationship can provide opportunities for individual and couple growth and fulfillment, and for acceptance and love, as each partner is known and loved by the other in an interdependent way (Mace and Mace, 1974b). Marriage is seen as a growing, dynamic, constantly changing relationship, based on "the dynamic interplay of the unique and changing needs, expectations, and skills of the two partners themselves" (Sherwood and Scherer, 1975, p. 14).

Luthman and Kirschenbaum (1974) have described the marital system as a dynamic complex of patterns of behaviors, ways of functioning, attitudes, feelings, norms, and so on, which exist between two married partners. Each believes these aspects are necessary in order for the relationship to function effectively and maintain a satisfactory equilibrium. A change in one aspect of the system is seen as having effects upon other aspects of the system.

Marital systems can be open or closed. An open system is receptive to change and able to change, and is open to alternative ways of responding to various facets of life. It respects and affirms the worth and value of differences, permits a wide range of feeling responses, and can make flexible adaptations to new inputs. A closed system resists change, has rigid qualities, values comformity and sees differences as a threat, does not value the expression of full range of feelings such as anger, tenderness, and sadness, and is relatively incapable of making flexible adaptations to new input.

A marital system tends to maintain a homeostatic balance between the two partners which permits stability that is needed for necessary tasks to be done and relationship needs to be addressed. However, too rigid a balance does not permit change to occur when it is needed for an individual or the relationship to grow.

Luthman and Kirschenbaum (1974) have also identified the following as important aspects of growth within an open system and well-functioning marital or family relationship: 1) appropriate feedback; 2) personality differences among family members viewed as exciting, rather than threatening; 3) conflict and disagreement are viewed and valued as a learning opportunity; 4) separation of internal intent from external manifestations; 5) ability to express feelings and perceptions, and to keep channels open for communication, intimacy, and growth.

Needless to say, such an open system, which the proponents of marriage enrichment value, does not happen by chance. They affirm the need for continued efforts on the part of both partners to keep the relationship viable over time, the need to be their own active agents of change rather than becoming victims of the change which occurs continually, and the need to develop the necessary interpersonal skills to make continued viability and creative change possible (Foote, 1963; Lederer and Jackson, 1968; Mace and Mace, 1975, 1977; Miller, Nunnally, and Wackman, 1976b; Otto, 1969).

ULTIMATE GOAL: THE INTENTIONAL COMPANIONSHIP MARRIAGE

For many people, there has been a change in the concept of marriage from a rigid and hierarchical institution to the concept of companionship marriage, which is a relationship based on intimacy, equality, and flexibility in interpersonal relationships (Mace and Mace, 1974b, 1975). We believe that the ultimate goal and underlying value of most marriage enrichment programs is the attainment and maintenance of such a relationship. We call it *intentional companionship marriage.*

Intentional companionship marriage is a relationship in which there is a strong commitment to an enduring marital dyad in which each person experiences increasing fulfillment and satisfaction. There is a strong emphasis on developing effective interpersonal relationships and on establishing and maintaining an open communication system. There is the ability to give and accept affection in an unconditional way, to accept the full range of feelings towards each other, to appreciate common interests and differences and accept and affirm each other's uniqueness, and to see each other as having equal status in the relationship.

There is a commitment to expanding and deepening the emotional aspects of the relationship, including the sexual dimension, and to developing and reinforcing marital strengths. This relationship is characterized by mutual affection, honesty, true intimacy, love, empathy, and understanding. There is an awareness of changing needs, desires, and aspirations, and appropriate responses to them. There is also a sense of self-worth in each partner and a balance between autonomy and interdependence, with each partner accepting equal responsibility for the success of the relationship.

The intentional companionship marriage is imbued with a conscious realization that marriage is not a static system with inflexible roles, but rather a dynamic, changing relationship, calling for continued commitment to openness, creative use of differences and conflict, negotiation and renegotiation of roles and norms, and continued individual and couple awareness and growth. In other words, there is an *intentional* commitment by both partners to work on the process of the relationship, and to develop the skills needed to insure the continued growth and vitality of the relationship.

Marriage enrichment practitioners use a variety of methods to help couples develop the acceptance, trust and skills needed to achieve such a relationship. Perhaps, we can say that the intentional companionship marriage is more of an ideal than a reality, perhaps even an unachievable goal. Yet, we believe it is the goal to which the marriage enrichment movement has committed itself. It is a continually developing and expanding goal, and in a real sense, the process of working towards the goal is the fulfillment of it!

EDUCATIONAL NATURE OF MARRIAGE ENRICHMENT

Proponents of marriage enrichment emphasize its dynamic, experiential, and educational nature (Buckland, 1977; Clinebell, 1976; Guerney, 1978; Mace and Mace, 1978; Otto, 1976; Sherwood and Scherer, 1975). Guerney (1977) describes an educational model as one in which attitudes and specific skills are taught in a structured and systematic fashion. Behavioral objectives are clearly stated, and appropriate evaluative measures are included in the program. A rationale is provided for what is to be learned, along with practice and supervision in developing skills and teaching participants to generalize beyond the learning situation to their everyday, life experiences. The focus is on setting goals and reaching them, increasing understanding, and creating a climate of growth and development. There is an emphasis on individual and relationship strengths, rather than on what is wrong with the relationship or how the relationship got to be where it is. There is a conscious avoidance of references to sickness or labels that have become associated with a medical model. To a greater or lesser degree, virtually all marriage enrichment programs follow such an educational model.

Harrell and Guerney (1976) have noted that research has shown that educational models can provide a successful structure for increasing interpersonal functioning. There is some agreement among professionals in the field of marital and family therapy that one of the goals of therapy is the education and re-education of the couple to facilitate their ability to relate interpersonally in a mutually satisfying way (Bach and Wyden, 1969; Rogers, 1972; Truax and Carkhuff, 1967). There is also an increasing tendency to use cognitive and experiential educational models in therapy. Such models include the identification of strengths as well as the learning of new skills in areas such as communication, problem solving, and conflict resolution. These findings support the rationale for using an educational approach in the marriage enrichment programs.

The educational nature and growth orientation of most marriage enrichment programs may appeal to a broader segment of the population than programs identified with counseling or therapy. Because of the stigma attached to these terms people may shy away from programs associated with them. However, education and skill training have positive connotations which could apply to any couple, and thus may have a broader appeal (Schauble and Hill, 1976).

PREVENTIVE NATURE OF MARRIAGE ENRICHMENT

Proponents of marriage enrichment also emphasize its preventive nature (Clinebell, 1976; Guerney, 1977; L'Abate, 1977a; Mace and Mace, 1975; Otto, 1976). That is, one aim is to prevent the emergence, development, or recurrence of interpersonal dysfunction. It is believed that by dealing with people in marriages which are basically functional, and by developing the potential and strengths that are there, growth and satisfaction can occur. As a positive, growth-oriented base develops, deterioration in the relationship can be halted or prevented. The parties learn how to recognize problems early, and how to cope with change and conflict. Of course, along with the preventive emphasis, there is a primary emphasis on increasing emotional and interpersonal satisfaction and on strengthening marriage and family life.

Eisenberg (1962), L'Abate (Note 2), and Sauber (1974) make reference to three possible levels of prevention. They are, primary prevention, which consists of promoting health, providing specific protection and the building of specific skills; secondary prevention, which focuses on early diagnosis and intervention to block further development of the dysfunction within the couple or family system; and tertiary prevention, where there is apparently irreversible dysfunction, and the focus is on limiting the spread of the dysfunction and promoting rehabilitation. The majority of marriage enrichment programs tend to fall in the primary prevention category (e.g., Clarke, 1970; Mace and Mace, 1975; Otto, 1976; Sauber, 1974). However, Guerney (1977) and L'Abate (1977a; Note 2), among others (e.g., Bolte, 1975; Gottman, Notarius, Gonso, and Markman, 1976; Schauble and Hill, 1976), have expanded into the areas of secondary prevention, by using enrichment programming as an adjunct to intensive marital and family therapy. Our program at the Marriage Council of Philadelphia is designed in this manner. (See Chapter 4, "Target Populations," for a discussion of the use of marriage enrichment with couples involved in therapy.)

It is an established fact that the need for mental health services far exceeds the number of qualified professionals available to give such services. In addition, the cost of such services is frequently prohibitive for couples and families in need. Clark Vincent (1973, 1977) and David and Vera Mace (1975) express the need for preventive mental health services to make a shift away from a pathological-remedial orientation to a preventive, experiential approach, emphasizing positive growth. They believe that such a shift will provide a better balance between the need and availability of mental health services because fewer people will be in need of such services. It is hoped that marriage enrichment will provide a needed and valuable service in the area of preventive marital health, and indeed, that is one of its major aims.

BALANCE BETWEEN RELATIONAL AND INDIVIDUAL GROWTH

Herbert Otto (1976) defines marriage enrichment in terms of "the development of marriage and individual potential while maintaining a consistent and primary focus on the relationship of the couple" (p. 14). His definition indicates the balance that most marriage enrichment programs try to provide between relational and marital growth on the one hand, and individual growth on the other.

Mace and Mace (1977) state that marriage enrichment programs need to focus on the simultaneous growth and development of the individual and of the marital relationship, with each aspect supporting the other. Such a focus contributes to the development of a growing, flexible, mutually satisfying relationship. Miller, Nunnally, and Wackman (1975) note that one goal of the Couples Communication Program is increased self-awareness, partner-awareness and couple-awareness, and increased self- and other-esteem. Otto (1969) speaks of actualizing the potential of the couple in relationship to each other and the personal potential of each individual in the relationship.

Travis and Travis (1975, 1976a) stress that self-actualization is needed along with relationship-actualization.

Most marriage enrichment programs emphasize the improvement of the marital relationship, devoting the majority of time to couple inter-action, improving couple communication, deepening the mutual acceptance and emotional life of the couple, fostering marriage strengths, and develop-ing marriage potential. At the same time, it is realized that acceptance, esteem, actualization, and expression of the self are crucial aspects of growth and development in the marriage and other relationships, and need to be addressed as well. Luthman and Kirschenbaum (1974) state that the "ideal base for a marital relationship is that each partner have a strong sense of himself as a separate, whole person, whose survival is attached to himself and to his own growth" (p. 110). They also stress the ability to be parents, chil-dren, and friends to each other as necessary to actualize the potential of the individual and the couple. Travis and Travis (1976a) speak of the need to grow individually together (p. 74), which implies personal growth, individu-ality, self-identity, and self-love as the base for relationship enhancement.

Some developers of marriage enrichment programs believe the marriage enrichment process should begin with the individual sense of fulfill-ment and worth. Others focus immediately on enhancement of the relation-ship and do not address the intrapsychic concerns of the individuals who form the participating dyad. Of course, in the latter instance, the climate of sharing, trust, empathy, and support contribute towards personal growth any-way. But, this is not the primary focus of such programs—the relationship between participating partners is.

We believe that marriage enrichment programs must respond to both individual and couple needs for growth and development. We believe that this can occur whether the program focuses equally on both individual and couple growth, or just primarily on enhancing the relationship. A prob-lem emerges only when one or the other is virtually excluded or ignored.

We have conducted unstructured interviews with several couples who have been enriched through participation in one of the more religiously oriented marriage enrichment programs. They reported what appears to be an absence of differentiation and individuation between partners, and a continu-ing attention to the enriched couple. We speculate that this consistent emphasis on unity, on the *we*, frequently results in a denial of the *me*, of the individual and his/her wants, needs and aspirations, which in turn can result in the denial of relationship problems and conflicts.

This is certainly not the avowed intention of the program, but is, nonetheless, an apparent reality for at least some of the participating couples. The emphasis, overt or covert, can be placed so much on *successfully* fulfill-ing the potential of the couple, and maintaining some ideal marital way of life, that the individual can be submerged or lost, and some real concerns and problems can be overlooked (Doherty, McCabe, and Ryder, 1978). The potential for future problems in such a relationship is obvious, regardless of the increased positive feeling, the new skills that may have been learned, or how much the couple has grown.

Many marriage enrichment practitioners emphasize the inevitability of conflict and the legitimacy of appropriately managed conflict within the marital relationship. Ther also stress that emerging conflict within a dynamic system is not always easily managed solely through dialogue and they frequently provide skill training in conflict management. However, many religious systems have emphasized self-denial for the greater good, and have viewed conflict as basically negative, relying on religious strength and spiritual values to overcome all problems. Practitioners of these systems may have difficulty moving beyond a verbal affirmation of the goals of marriage enrichment regarding the central place of individual growth and effective conflict utilization. Yet, what is needed is application and practice of what is verbally stated.

This criticism of one particular aspect of some of the religiously oriented marriage enrichment programs (though emphatically not all of them) is a reminder that a potentially valuable idea is not immune to distortion. Constant self-criticism, evaluation, empirical research, and receptivity to feedback are needed to correct such misrepresentations when they appear, and to guard against their development or return.

The Process of Marriage Enrichment

THEORETICAL FOUNDATION

An examination of the process of marriage enrichment needs to be preceded by a discussion of the theoretical foundation on which both the process and the programs are built. Many marriage enrichment programs are eclectic, in that they draw from a variety of contributors and theoretical frameworks, such as those outlined by Satir, Perls, Frankl, Rogers, and Berne. However, eclectic seems to be used by some practitioners as synonomous with "hodgepodge" or "smorgasbord," and to cover for, or rationalize away, the lack of a well-developed theoretical framework. We can only hope that more proponents of marriage enrichment will acknowledge the need to develop and clearly state a theoretical base for their programs as Guerney (1977) and Miller et al. (1976b) have done.

Humanistic psychology which emerged and flourished in the 1960s can be seen as a precursor to the marriage enrichment movement. This psychology, which espouses the expression of feelings, creating effective relationships, and fulfilling personal potential, is the inspiration for marriage enrichment. All else grows from the idea that each person has an inherent tendency towards growth and self-actualization, with respect to self and others. This human potential movement also helped to make our society aware of the benefits of group experiences and techniques, an important aspect of the marriage enrichment process.

Building on these basic concepts, Bernard Guerney is one of the few proponents of marriage enrichment to have established a clear and specific theoretical base for his program (Relationship Enhancement Programs). He has carefully developed the elements of Rogerian psychotherapy, behavior modification (operant learning theory), and social learning theory. These same elements, as well as group process theory, expressed or not, appear to form the foundation of virtually all marriage enrichment programs, as well as group process theory, all of which are discussed in the following paragraphs.

Rogerian psychotherapy affirms the importance of the emotional life and self-concept of the individual, as well as the important effects inter-personal relations have upon these intrapsychic dimensions. Complete acceptance and respect for the participants is emphasized, and acceptance of negative as well as positive feelings (Guerney, 1977). In marriage enrichment programming, there is an emphasis on providing an empathic environment in which participants can freely express their feelings and experience increased self-acceptance and knowledge, and increased acceptance of others and from others, especially their marital partner. Leader congruence and modeling of empathic behavior is also stressed. The assumption is made that all of this will contribute to changes in cognition and the attitudes which underlie behavior (Guerney, 1977), and will lead the participants to change their behavior.

Behavior modification approaches which have incorporated social learning theory with modeling and behavior rehearsal, and which recognize the importance of reeducation in the area of cognitive functions as well as the more traditional behavioral functions, are also utilized. Marriage enrichment frequently is less specific than traditional behavior modification and has more general goals, such as increased interpersonal effectiveness, increased intimacy, and relationship enhancement. However, along with these general goals, many programs also have very specific behavioral goals, such as the Relationship Enhancement Program, (Guerney, 1977) the Couples Communication Program, (Miller et al., 1976b) and Marriage Encounter (Bosco, 1973). Other program developers do not clearly state their specific behavioral objectives but employ a variety of behavioral methods and techniques within the program. To a greater or lesser degree, virtually all marriage enrichment programs use techniques such as modeling, behavior rehearsal, prompting, and reinforcement. In some programs, they are systematically employed as instructional methods, as in Guerney and Miller, while in others they are employed in nonsystematic ways.

Behaviorally speaking, most marriage enrichment experiences appear to be designed to accelerate behaviors perceived to be desirable and rewarding in the marriage relationship (e.g., positive statements, ownership and expression of feelings, effective negotiation skills). Some programs virtually prohibit the expression of negative statements or feelings, apparently with the belief that a deceleration of negative verbal and affective exchanges, plus an acceleration of positive verbal, behavioral, and affective exchanges, will lead to the elimination of undesirable and dysfunctional behaviors.

Marriage enrichment is clearly indebted to Skinner (1953, 1969) for his emphasis on social reinforcement, an important aspect of behavior modification approaches. However, proponents view the significance of such reinforcement in the learning process as secondary to repeated practice and modeled demonstrations. In marriage enrichment, the main contribution of social reinforcement may be in the increasing of the positive feelings participants have regarding themselves, which thus keeps motivation high to improve and develop effective relationship skills (Guerney, 1977).

Proponents of marriage enrichment believe that people can learn new interaction skills and can correct deficiencies in social learning. For example, people who have never learned how to manage conflict can be taught to do so. Deficiencies in social learning are thus viewed as important components in relationship discord, and the learning and continued practice of appropriate skills is viewed as an important component in marital and relationship health.

In addition to Rogerian psychotherapy, behavior modification and social learning theory, group process theory must also be mentioned as one of the foundation blocks of marriage enrichment. The group experience is seen as providing a temporary and safe learning environment through which trust can grow, and from which support can be drawn. In such an environment, couples can observe alternative models of relating as they observe other couples interacting. They learn and practice interactional skills, and how to give and receive positive feedback among peers (Miller et al., 1976b). In addition, participants have the opportunity to consult with and help other couples (altruism) and to experience a sense of universality.

More specifically, Irvin Yalom (1970) has identified the following as primary categories of curative factors in group therapy: 1) imparting information; 2) instillation of hope; 3) universality (sense of "I am not alone with this problem"); 4) altruism (helping other group members through support, reassurance, etc.); 5) corrective recapitulation of the primary family group; 6) development of socializing techniques (social learning); 7) imitative behavior (modeling); 8) interpersonal learning; 9) group cohesiveness (sense of solidarity, we-ness, experiencing the group as a source of strength and encouragement); and 10) catharsis (ventilation of positive and negative feelings). These curative factors are interdependently operative in every type of therapy group, including couples groups, but they have varying degrees of importance depending on the nature, goals, and composition of the specific group.

Mace (1975a) reminds us that a marriage enrichment group is not just a group of unrelated individuals, but a group of subgroups, "each of which is a pre-existing and ongoing social unit" (p. 171), making for a more complex group process. He further reminds us that enrichment groups are different from therapy groups and comparisons between the two require careful analysis. A proper comparison awaits appropriate empirical research. However, virtually these same curative factors have been identified by Egan (1970) as being operative in all growth-oriented group experiences (with the exception of the corrective recapitulation of the primary family group). His list includes these common elements of growth groups: 1) opportunity to present and reveal the way a participant sees things, feels, etc.; 2) climate of experimentation; 3) feedback; 4) supportive atmosphere; 5) cognitive map; 6) practice; 7) planning application of new learnings to everyday life; 8) relearning how to learn; 9) emphasis on effective communication and emotional or affective learning; 10) participative leadership; 11) normal populations; and 12) the use of structured experiences.

To a greater or lesser degree, we believe these curative factors and common elements are present in marriage enrichment groups as well. The curative factors provide the rationale for the use of group experiences in marriage enrichment programming. However, as Yalom noted, the curative factors will have varying degrees of importance depending on the nature, goals, and composition of a specific group or program. For example, at one end of the continuum would be the Marriage Encounter program which focuses almost entirely on dyadic interaction, with group process being limited to the experiencing of several presentations by the leadership team in the total group setting, shared meals, and a religious service. In such a group setting, many of the curative factors would not be overtly operative. Yet the sense of universality and vicarious support the participants can experience, as they realize everyone has gathered for the same purpose, has been reported by many couples. In addition, follow-up sharing groups which meet on a regular basis following the initial weekend experience provide the opportunity for more of the curative factors to be experienced.

On the other end of the continuum would be the program model used by the Maces (1976b). This model involves a minimum of organization and structure, and the group of couples meeting for a weekend experience decide for themselves what the agenda and goals will be. Needless to say, in such a relatively unstructured group setting, more of the curative factors would be overtly operative. Mace (1975b) even suggests that leaders in such groups serve as models and surrogate parents (p. 40), which, in this case, even would suggest Yalom's idea of corrective recapitulation of the primary family group.

In summary, the theoretical bases of the process of marriage enrichment are: the broad base of humanistic psychology, Rogerian psychotherapy, behavior modification and social learning theory, and group process theory. These form the foundation from which all other aspects of the process of marriage enrichment emerge. We believe the essential particulars of this process are its ongoing nature and positive emphasis, the use of confrontation, the emphasis on developing communications skills, and the experience of self-disclosure, all which will be developed in the following sections of this chapter.

THE ONGOING NATURE OF MARRIAGE ENRICHMENT

Marriage enrichment has frequently been identified with weekend-long programs, or time-limited, marital growth groups, which meet, for example, once a week for six to eight weeks, two to four hours each meeting. Many couples initially experience marriage enrichment through such a program, and come to view that experience as an important part of their growth. However, the process of marriage enrichment is an ongoing one not restricted to participation in weekend experiences or time-limited groups. Many practitioners and participants emphasize that such participation is a beginning, not an end, to the process of marital and relationship growth and enhancement (Mace and Mace, 1976a, 1978). Couples participating in a basic program can be introduced to certain skills. They can gain a sense of the potential of their relationship and can perceive the need for change and growth. However, more and more leaders are emphasizing the need for an ongoing support system or time-limited group, with continued growth experiences after the initial experience (Hopkins, et al., 1978; Mace, 1975b; Otto, 1976; Rappaport, 1976). Such follow-up groups would provide support, encouragement, and positive reinforcement and feedback. There would be further opportunities to learn and practice interactional skills, and opportunities to give and receive help. Without such a support system, it is believed that gains from the initial experience quickly fade. Clinebell (1975) believes that a variety of marriage enrichment programs are needed for different points in the life span, and it is clear that he sees marriage enrichment as a life-long process.

Emphasis on the ongoing process of marriage enrichment reflects the idea that established and entrenched patterns of marital interaction do not change overnight or by participation in one program. It is also based on the belief that self-help programs, by themselves, are not sufficient to produce enduring change. It is believed that a couple must make a commitment to work at enhancing the relationship continually. They must also decide to become involved with other couples who are committed to the same goal by joining an ongoing program of growth, be it an ongoing growth group or special-interest groups in areas such as decision making, parenting, or sexuality. The process may even include the use of regular, preventive, marital checkups (even if nothing may be wrong in the relationship) as a means of identifying assets and strengths as well as areas where improvement is needed. Competent third-party consultation can be helpful, but individuals, couples, or groups of couples could do their own checkups as well. It is also conceivable that marriage or relationship counseling will be needed when individual, couple, or support group resources are insufficient to enable a couple to move through a blockage in the relationship.

POSITIVE EMPHASIS OF MARRIAGE ENRICHMENT

A review of several programs shows that marriage enrichment has a decided emphasis upon the positive aspects of the marital relationship (Clinebell, 1975; Mace and Mace, 1977; Otto, 1972, 1976). There is also the belief that identifying and sharing positive aspects with each other can generate a highly satisfying emotional experience for both partners and even make it possible for negative feelings to be expressed in ways that can lead to goal-setting behavior (Clarke, 1970; Mace and Mace, 1976b). We wonder too if there are not some long-term benefits which accrue to the couple after such a highly satisfying emotional experience. It would seem possible that a sense of hope, and remembrances of loving, positive exchanges could be drawn upon in times of pain or distress, perhaps serving as a motivation to overcome current difficulties. Those memories of what was once experienced may help to achieve a level of needed intimacy.

The positive emphasis provides a base for moving to more sensitive and difficult issues, such as those involving conflict or anger (Liberman, Wheeler, and Sanders, 1976). The teaching of specific skills, which makes the expression and constructive resolution of negative feelings possible, is also a part of many programs (Guerney, 1977). However, some programs deal only with affirmation and do not focus on potential areas of conflict such as unfulfilled wants and needs. Such an approach raises serious questions about how people who receive training only in the expression of positive feelings and thoughts can be expected to express themselves effectively with negative feelings and thoughts in conflicted situations. Couples need practice in both areas, and this belief has led many facilitators to include components that deal with the expression of negative feelings and conflict resolution in their programs (e.g., Guerney, 1977; Mace and Mace, 1976b; Sherwood and Scherer, 1975).

CONFRONTATION IN MARRIAGE ENRICHMENT PROGRAMS

Mace and Mace (1974b) and Otto (1976) note that most marriage enrichment program leaders do not utilize, encourage, or even permit pressure to elicit sharing or self-disclosure. Nor is confrontation utilized, encouraged, or permitted to expose behavior or to attempt to force a change in behavior. Marriage enrichment programs operating from a Gestalt perspective (*e.g.,* Zinker and Leon, 1976) appear to be the one consistent exception to this rule or norm. These programs incorporate criticism as well as strong confrontation.

We believe that program leaders do well to prevent irresponsible confrontation (*e.g.,* telling people off), which can be destructive to relationship and individual growth. However, responsible confrontation can have beneficial results (Egan, 1970). Responsible confrontation involves a caring invitation to the person to examine, and if appropriate, modify his or her behavior, in order to improve the ability to relate with others. Needless to say, this is quite different from what many people have learned through their experiences with confrontation. The concept of nondemanding requests for behavioral change is a foreign idea. The concept of care as an element of responsible confrontation is also alien. The idea of confronting behavior, and not motivation, is new for many people, as is Egan's idea of confronting strengths, or potential strengths, as well as weaknesses. (An example of a confrontation of unused potential would be the following: "You rarely share your feelings directly with me, but when you do, I feel closer to you. I wish you would do it more often.")

Responsible confrontation (Egan, 1970) requires that the confronter consider, in advance, the following: 1) motives of the confrontation; 2) the potential impact upon the confrontee at this point in time; 3) the needs, sensitivity, and capabilities of the confrontee as well as the confronter; and 4) that the confrontation occur only if there is a genuine desire to work towards creative change, as opposed to a desire to punish.

Marriage enrichment program designers and leaders must realize that responsible confrontation is not antithetical to support, caring, and warmth. They must also be careful not to ignore the very real need that people have to learn effective confrontation skills as part of effective conflict utilization. If this need is ignored, gains from increasing positive expressions may be offset when the inevitable negative expressions occur. Or, individuals and couples may move to a position of denying the reality of conflict and avoiding requests for behavioral change in order to avoid irresponsible confrontation and the feared expression of negative feelings. It would be better to teach couples how to rechannel conflict and confrontation into a positive experience, albeit one that is frequently painful. This positive approach to conflict utilization and confrontation is addressed by several marriage enrichment programs (e.g., Guerney, 1977).

EMPHASIS ON COMMUNICATION

The content of marriage enrichment programs varies greatly, but most programs emphasize the need to communicate effectively (L'Abate, 1977a; Mace and Mace, 1974b, 1975; Otto, 1976). Seventy-seven percent of enrichment leaders surveyed by Otto (1975, 1976) indicated that an average of more than half of the time spent in the program was devoted to the development of communication skills. Many participants have indicated that the training they received in effective communication and emotional expression has been extremely valuable to them as individuals and as a couple.

It can be said that the heart of marriage enrichment is couple communication or dialogue (Mace and Mace, 1977; Regula, 1975). Specifically, that means effective, deep sharing of feelings, thoughts, wants, needs, and intentions between partners. This is a learned process which is cultivated intentionally, and practiced with discipline, rather than a one time only experience. In some programs, this dialogue takes place between partners in total privacy (e.g., Marriage Encounter: Bosco, 1973). In other programs, couple dialogue in a group setting is believed to be helpful (e.g., ACME model: Mace and Mace, 1976b). The aim is for couples to be able to experience "total human expression" with each other (Egan, 1970). That means, marriage enrichment seeks to teach partners how to communicate fully on an intellectual and emotional level, both verbally and nonverbally, in a way that permits emotions to be appropriately allied with rational expression.

Another goal is for couples to learn how to give and receive supportive behavior. It is an acknowledged fact that an atmosphere which is conducive to, and actively encourages growth, is helpful and needed for that growth to occur. In other words, people must feel supported in their efforts to grow. Egan (1970) strongly believes the prerequisite of supportive behavior is total listening, one of the core concepts of communications training. Total listening involves listening to all of the cues emitted by the other person, listening with one's ears, eyes, mind, heart, imagination, and even one's touch. It involves listening to words and feelings, and being alert to hidden or coded messages. It involves listening to one's self as well as the other person, and it is an objective and subjective process. As Lief (1977) has suggested, total listening includes: 1) self awareness, or sensitivity to one's own feelings and thoughts and behaviors; 2) empathy, or sensitivity to the other person; 3) "recipathy, or sensitivity to one's own feelings in response to the behaviors or words of the other person" (p. 289); and 4) impact-awareness, a "sensitivity to the impact of one's own words or behavior on the other person." (p. 289)

Egan (1970) believes that reinforcement for growth-producing behavior also involves the following: 1) a necessary degree of warmth; 2) unconditional positive regard, or genuine, nonjudgmental acceptance (not necessarily approval) of the other person; 3) affirmation of the universality of our human experience (feelings, successes, failures, etc.); 4) physical and psychological availability to each other; 5) congruent interactions; 6) trust in one's self and in the other person; and 7) appropriate recognition of the contributions and behavior of others and appropriate responses to them.

Total human expression and supportive behavior are thus seen as integral parts of effective communication. And, clearly, effective communication is positively linked with marital adjustment and satisfaction, as well as increased self- and other-acceptance (Alexander, 1973; Collins, 1977; Epstein and Jackson, 1978; Jacobson and Martin, 1976; Olson, 1976; Rappaport, 1976). Navran (1967) showed a positive correlation between marital adjustment and the ability to communicate, suggesting that couples can improve their relationship by focusing on how they communicate and by improving their skills in this area. He also attempted to clarify the often fuzzy term "open communication." He found that happily married couples talked more to each other, conveyed the feeling that they understood what was being said to them, had a wide range of subjects available to them, preserved communication channels, showed more sensitivity to each other's feelings, personalized their language symbols, and made more use of supplementary nonverbal techniques of communication.

In view of the increasing evidence which relates effective communication to effective marital functioning and satisfaction, it is easy to see why marriage enrichment programs place such a heavy emphasis upon communications training. The emphasis is based on several beliefs: that individuals and couples need to learn how to communicate effectively, that they can learn new skills and make needed changes through practice and feedback in a supportive, experimental, and experiential setting, that they can then transfer their learnings to everyday situations, and that such a joint effort builds self and couple esteem and relationship satisfaction (Bolte, 1975; Miller, Corrales, and Wackman, 1975).

Many marriage enrichment programs rely on the communications theories of Satir (1965, 1967, 1972); Watzlawick, Beavin, and Jackson (1967); Berne (1964, 1968); Gordon (1970); and Miller, Nunnally, and Wackman (1975, 1976b). In virtually all programs, the focus is on the present, and on the process of communication and interaction as well as the content. Leaders model the skills to be learned. Skills and concepts are taught in a supportive atmosphere, emphasis is placed on awareness of interaction patterns, and skills are developed and practiced in a dyad, while focusing on important issues and using supportive feedback from other participants. Some programs make use of homework assignments to facilitate the integration of new skills and the transfer of learnings to everyday situations (Miller, 1975). The research of Goldstein (1973), McLeish, Matheson, and Park (1973), Jacobson and Martin (1976), among others, suggests that such a combination of experiential, didactic-cognitive, and modeling techniques is the most effective way to teach couples new communication skills (L'Abate, 1977a).

Some enrichment programs are specifically oriented towards skill training. That is, they focus on the development of a particular set of communication and interaction skills (e.g., Couples Communication Program: Miller et al., 1976b; Relationship Enhancement Program: Guerney, 1977). It has been suggested that participation in such a program is a helpful precursor to, or adjunct to, participation in one of the more broadly based, open-ended, or issue-oriented marriage enrichment programs (Guerney, 1977; Hopkins et al., 1978; Mace and Mace, 1976a). These skill-training programs can teach participants how to develop basic skills which are needed to explore other areas and content issues. Basically, the skills focus on honest, open communication, the ability to express feelings, desires, and thoughts, and the ability to respond in an empathic manner.

In the more broadly based programs, the specific skill-training emphasis is often absent or less heavily emphasized. In such programs, the content of what is shared appears to be valued as highly as the process, and there is emphasis on attitudinal changes in the relationship. In the Marriage Encounter program, a specific, but limited, method of dialogue is practiced (Genovese, 1975). In the model suggested by the Association of Couples for Marriage Enrichment (ACME), (Mace and Mace, 1976a), there is a minimum of organization and structure; the skills which are taught and practiced emerge from the expressed needs of the group of couples meeting for that particular period of time.

Obviously, there is much overlapping among the various programs in the area of communications. The distinction is a matter of emphasis—on the type of training, the specific skills to be learned, and the degree of structure by which the skills are taught. Of course, proponents of each method are able to defend their approach, some with more research support than others (e.g., Guerney, 1977; Miller et al., 1976b). Some of the more broadly based and more popular programs have not yet been adequately researched, and overall, the number of relevant studies on marriage enrichment is very small. (See Chapter 5, Research on Marriage Enrichment.)

Epstein and Jackson (1978), reporting on a specific and systematic communication training program they developed, suggest that it may be easier to implement behavioral rather than attitudinal changes in close interpersonal relationships. Their suggestion leads us to raise a series of questions. Should participation in a sharply focused communication training program precede a more broadly based, issue-oriented marriage enrichment program? Would this enable the participants to gain more from the latter experience by having already increased their basic communication skills? Or, should participation in the more broadly based program precede the communication-skill training? Would this sequence generate a high level of positive feeling which might increase the commitment to a sharply focused communication training program? Or, is the sequence irrelevant? Or, do both have to occur, perhaps even simultaneously, for stable, enduring, positive behavioral and attitudinal change to occur between partners? Only appropriate research, as yet undone, can enlighten this issue.

In conclusion, proponents of marriage enrichment view training in communication skills as an important part of programming, though they implement such training in greatly varied ways. The mastering of communication skills of itself is not viewed as a panacea. However, in combination with a spirit of good will and a commitment to the goals of marriage enrichment, communication training stands out as an important contribution to relationship enhancement.

SELF-DISCLOSURE

Self-disclosure—the revealing of one's thoughts and feelings to another person—is of central significance to the philosophy and process of marriage enrichment. Several studies have been conducted which show that self-disclosure is most effective when it is appropriate, honest, direct, explicit, and congruent. In addition, when there is a balance between the expression of thoughts and feelings, the disclosure takes on an even greater meaning (Derlega and Chaikin, 1975; Egan, 1970; Gilbert, 1976; Jourard, 1964, 1971; Luft, 1969).

According to Luft, self-disclosure is appropriate and most helpful when the following criteria are met: 1) when it is a function of the ongoing relationship; 2) when it occurs reciprocally; 3) when it is timely; 4) when it is pertinent; 5) when it moves by relatively small increments; 6) when it can be confirmed by the other person; 7) when account is taken of the effect disclosure has on the other person; 8) when it creates a reasonable risk; 9) when it accelerates during a crisis; and 10) when the content is mutually shared (Luft, 1969; pp. 132–133).

Self-disclosure exerts its influence on relationships in several ways. First, one gains a greater awareness of true self through successful disclosure (Jourard, 1964, 1971). Second, self-disclosure helps an individual discern similarities and differences between his perceptions and feelings and those of others. It also makes it possible for people to learn directly from each other what their specific needs, expectations, and intentions are. Thus, self-disclosure encourages people to redirect their perceptions of others from roles such as husband, wife, mother or father, to unique sensitive individuals. Third, self-disclosure and self-esteem are apparently positively related (Gilbert, 1976). In other words, the higher the self-esteem, the higher the level of self-disclosure. Finally, disclosure begets more disclosure (Jourard and Richman, 1963), but a climate of trust and acceptance is needed to initiate and maintain the reciprocating cycle.

Although the benefits of self-disclosure cannot be disputed, the philosophy of marriage enrichment does not endorse unlimited disclosure. It is limited to the extent that it be positive and voluntary, and not the result of confrontation. These limitations are supported by research. Evidence suggests that the valence of a disclosure (its positiveness or negativeness) may be more important than the level of intimacy achieved (Gilbert and Horenstein, 1975). That means that high levels of disclosure actually may be destructive if the thoughts and feelings disclosed are highly negative.

The research also suggests that there is a point at which further disclosure *reduces* satisfaction within a relationship (Cozby, 1973; Gilbert, 1976). Therefore, it is important to match couples with varying self-disclosure needs and abilities to the appropriate program. For example, if a relatively low-disclosing couple participates in a program where the norm is for high disclosure in a group setting, that couple may feel pressured to disclose themselves beyond the point that is optimal for their growth and development. Or, the couple may emotionally withdraw from the experience out of anxiety and the need to maintain their defenses.

A fact of life for some couples is that security needs may outweigh their needs for relationship depth. If pressured too much, the potential benefits of a marriage enrichment program may be reduced or lost accordingly. In fact, negative results may even occur. But, if couples participate in a program with disclosure norms that match or slightly exceed their own, their security needs probably would be met. Within this trusting environment, they also would be encouraged to work at the growing edges of their relationship, increasing self-disclosure at their own rate, thereby experiencing new depths of intimacy. Conversely, a relatively high-disclosing couple participating in a program that has a norm of low disclosure may be extremely frustrated in their growth by the rigidity and inflexibility of the structure, the low level of disclosure, and the inability to share and disclose with other couples.

Another argument for limited disclosure in marriage enrichment programs is that at the high risk end of the continuum, some couples are not able to survive in-depth examination and disclosure regarding information, disappointments, and conflicts (Gilbert, 1976). For some couples, the desire for intimate commitment and the ability to risk are such that they will go to great lengths to achieve their potential in this area. Other couples, however, may desire a different degree of intimate commitment, or may not have the same capacity for risk. These couples may need to avoid certain or most aspects of disclosure at the high risk end of the continuum. This does not mean that they are less competent or open than other couples. They are simply different in this respect, and will need to be encouraged to discover and develop their own kind of intimacy.

What is needed in marriage enrichment programming is a response to the varying disclosure needs of all couples. There is also a need for clear, public expression of disclosure norms and possibilities that are likely to occur within the framework of a particular program model. Such a statement of norms would make it easier, and less a matter of chance, for a particular couple to select or be referred to a program which could suitably address their perceived needs and risk-level.

In summary, marriage enrichment emphasizes certain key aspects of self-disclosure and sees them as integral parts of a mutually satisfying and growing relationship. They are: that the disclosure be voluntary, positive, not the result of confrontation, and accented on the building of self-esteem. These attitudes are theoretically sound and supported by the research literature on self-disclosure. In other words, if disclosure occurs within this framework, which also emphasizes commitment, intimacy, and acceptance of each other, it would appear that it serves the function of deepening the relationship between the persons involved.

Marriage Enrichment Programs

⌖ **3**

Marriage enrichment can take place in a variety of formal or informal settings, but the two most common time formats are: the intensive retreat, conference, or marathon which can last from a weekend to a five-day experience, with the weekend being most common, or a series of weekly meetings in the form of either a marital growth group or a couple communication program (Hopkins et al., 1978; Mace and Mace, 1974b). Many couples experience both types of programs.

INTENSIVE WEEKEND PROGRAMS

The intensive weekend experience has the advantage of providing participants with the opportunity to be together as a couple, away from normal routines, commitments, and pressures, in an atmosphere of seclusion and leisure. They are able to take a continuous and intensive look at the marriage relationship, working with other couples on enhancing the relationship (Mace and Mace, 1974). However, if there is no ongoing follow-up and support group provided after the initial experience, the shock of return to the realities of everyday life can be somewhat painful, leaving the couple with a feeling of isolation. In such a situation, positive gains from the weekend experience can quickly fade, and integration of learnings and skills frequently does not occur.

Programs with the intensive weekend format vary in their degree of structure and focus on the couple. The continuum ranges from highly-structured and couple-centered, to relatively nonstructured and couple-group centered.

At one end of this continuum is the Marriage Encounter model (Bosco, 1973), in which total group interaction is limited to the sharing of meals and religious services. There is no sharing of marital experiences be-

29

tween couples or in the total group, except by the leadership couple. The leadership couple, working with a trained religious leader, make several presentations to the total group, after which each couple, in the privacy of their own room, write down their personal reflections upon a variety of personal, interpersonal, and spiritual issues (I, We, We-God, We-God-World). Following the writing, each partner reads what the other has written, and each encourages the other to verbally develop and further describe the written feelings, in an attempt to experience each other more fully at an affective level. This specific dialogue process is repeatedly practiced throughout the weekend. The opportunity is provided for participants to join ongoing support groups after the initial experience, and couples are encouraged to continue the process of daily dialogue. This model has also been adapted for engaged couples.

Highly structured, couple-centered programs such as Marriage Encounter involve less anxiety over public disclosure than programs with more focus on the couple-group. However, the couple-centered programs do not provide the possibility for potentially valuable observer feedback and support in the presence of other couples, which frequently occurs following the modeling of the leadership couple or other participant couples in the other programs (L'Abate, 1977a; cf. Luft, 1969; Yalom, 1970).

Near the middle of the structured versus nonstructured continuum are programs such as the Marriage Communication Lab (Mace and Mace, 1976b; Smith and Smith, 1976). Various issues and aspects of the marital relationship are addressed through a series of experiential and affective exercises, theoretical input, total group interaction, and skill practice and couple dialogue within a small group setting (five to six couples). This type of structure, which involves interaction between and within dyads, provides the possibility for the giving and receiving of potentially valuable observer feedback and support. The intention is to create a supportive and trusting environment, with little or no confrontation, so that individuals and couples can feel free to risk self-disclosure and become vulnerable to each other in the presence of other persons. This frequently occurs, following the modeling of the leadership couple or other participant couples. Even within this trusting environment, however, some people are too anxious to reveal their true thoughts and feelings. Instead, they may attempt to present themselves or their relationships in an overly positive way, and thus, truly intimate self-disclosure may never take place (L'Abate, 1977a).

At the unstructured end of the continuum is the program used by the Maces (1976b, 1977). This program shares much in common with the other two models, but there is a minimum of organization and structure (Mace and Mace, 1976b). A particular group of couples, usually five to eight couples per leadership team, meet for a prescribed period of time, and establish their own goals and agenda. The group stays together, except for an occasional private couple dialogue. Although a few structured exercises may be used, much of the time is devoted to couple dialogue, that is, husband and wife talking and sharing together in the presence of other couples. This model provides the possibility for the giving and receiving of observer feedback, support, and encouragement. The lack of a structured agenda may lead to the avoidance or neglect of certain key issues in marital interaction. However, that need not be a detriment, since this is viewed as only an initial experience, and one which will be followed by other learning experiences.

MULTIWEEK PROGRAMS

Multiweek marital enrichment experiences have the advantage of allowing participant couples the opportunity of spaced learning and continuing reinforcement for a number of weeks. These programs also provide the opportunity for doing homework between meetings and for the practice of new skills within the context of an ongoing support group (Mace and Mace, 1974b). Disadvantages of the multiweek format are the possibility of a lack of intensity, broken continuity, or the contamination of the process by the normal routines and responsibilities of daily life.

Some multiweek programs give homework assignments for the couples to do at home between meetings. This allows them to practice and reinforce what they have learned in the sessions. The assignments involve reading and skill practice, and focus on positive feelings and experiences, effectively serving as positive reinforcement for the behaviors of each partner (Schauble and Hill, 1976).

Research on this subject suggests that the use of homework with couples in therapy has positive effects upon their marital relationship (L'Abate, 1977a; Paul and Paul, 1975; Shelton and Ackerman, 1974). The recent research of L'Abate (1977a) concurrently suggests that an enrichment program, combined with couple work at home between sessions, results in a higher percentage of positive change than does participation in the enrichment program alone.

As with the intensive experiences, there is a variety of multiweek models and programs. In general, however, the many multiweek programs can be classified as either marital growth groups or couple communication training programs.

The program content of marital growth groups is commonly the same as the content of intensive weekend programs with the difference being in the weekly time format. As with the weekend experiences, the marital growth groups may vary in the degree of structure and focus on the couple. These programs are conducted on a weekly basis to provide the various aforementioned advantages to the participants. The weekly marital enrichment group may be time-limited or open-ended. Marital groups which do not use leadership couples who meet the criteria of ACME for certification are called *support groups* by ACME. The term *marital growth group* is reserved by ACME for groups which are more formally organized and are led by ACME certified couples (Hopkins et. al., 1978).

Many of the communication skills training programs meet once a week, for one to four hours, for five to eight weeks (e.g., Relationship Enhancement Programs: Guerney, 1977; MARDILAB: Stein, 1975; Couples Communication Program: Miller et al., 1976b). These programs are generally highly structured and behaviorally oriented. They are based on the hypothesis that marital relationships can be enhanced through the use of short-term, highly structured, behaviorally oriented group experiences and programs. This hypothesis has received some support by the research of Rappaport (1976) and Phillips and Wiener (1966).

Two of the most widely used communications training programs are the Relationship Enhancement Program (Guerney, 1977) and the Couples Communication Program (Miller, Nunnally, and Wackman, 1975, 1976b; Nunnally, Miller, and Wackman, 1975).The goal of the Couples Communication Program is to help people improve communication in a relationship (not necessarily a marital relationship), from a stance of equality, intimacy, and openness, so that meaning and growth are maintained. Two kinds of skills are developed: 1) self- and other-awareness skills, so that partners can understand their feelings, thoughts, intentions, rules, norms, and patterns of interacting, and 2) communication skills, to help participants modify their rules, norms, and patterns of interacting, so as to keep the system flexible and viable. The program is structured, with specific goals, and employs experiential learning through exercises, readings, lectures, small group discussion, and repeated skill practice in groups and through homework between sessions. The format frequently involves five to seven couples, meeting for three hours, one night per week for four consecutive weeks, with a trained instructor.

The Relationship Enhancement Program (Guerney, 1977) and the Conjugal Relationship Enhancement Program (Rappaport, 1976) are highly structured, short-term, educational models for improving communication, enhancing personal and marital relationships, and for preventing problems which could arise within them. All of the Relationship Enhancement Programs employ and emphasize Rogerian, client-centered, therapeutic principles, including direct expression of feelings and empathic listening. Concepts and specific skills are taught through didactic and experiential-modeling methods, and they are practiced within each session and at home between sessions. Skills taught include the following: 1) recognizing feelings, desires, and motivations in oneself and in others; 2) learning to express oneself honestly and congruently; 3) learning how to respond to others with understanding and acceptance; and 4) learning how to help others to behave in a similar fashion. Program formats range from weekend marathon groups to a series of one-hour, weekly meetings. The program is designed for use with individuals, couples, families, as well as groupings of these, and other client and professional groupings.

Rappaport and Harrell (1975) use an educational, behavioral exchange model to implement their Conjugal Relationship Enhancement Program (Guerney, 1977; Rappaport, 1976), and see it as being effective *after* a married couple has learned specific, effective communication skills. The goal of their program is to enable motivated and willing couples to resolve marital conflict more effectively. This is accomplished through the teaching of specific reciprocal exchange and bargaining skills, which are based on the assumption that both partners have resources of value to the other. From the beginning of the program, participants are encouraged to utilize their own resources and to negotiate their own contracts. The leader-educator-therapist is thus not the architect of change, but a facilitator of change.

This model differs from most marriage enrichment programs in that it starts with a problem-focus and the identification of undesirable behaviors, and then moves to a positive restatement of them. Generally speaking, marriage enrichment programs start with an emphasis on the identification and expression of positive behaviors and feelings. However, the educational nature of this model (i.e., skills are taught), the immediate use of the couples' resources, and the underlying assumption that they are capable of accomplishing the task, all of which are foundation stones of the growth model, link this program to other marriage enrichment programs.

Many other multiweek models have been developed, including the Marriage Diagnostic Laboratory or MARDILAB (Stein, 1975), the Pairing Enrichment Program (Travis and Travis, 1975; 1976a), and the reciprocity-counseling-behavioral approach of Dixon and Sciara (1977).

L'Abate (1977a) and Guerney (1977) note that their particular enrichment models can be used with one couple at a time or in the more common format involving a group of couples. L'Abate's view is that "enrichment programs are a structured, manual-directed, already written and presented approach that is based on a linear model of information processing following incremental, additive, progressive and step-wise presentation of information to be used by couples and families" (1977a, p. 214). He describes program designs for couples and families in areas such as confronting change, problem-solving skills for dating couples, sexuality and sensuality, man-woman relations, assertiveness, equality, reciprocity training, negotiation, conflict resolution, becoming parents, effective parenting, single-parent families, widowhood, and death and dying (L'Abate and Collaborators, 1975). He has also developed a system of classification for his enrichment programs based on the following approaches: affective versus cognitive, practical versus theoretical, simple versus complex, general versus specific, and structured versus developmental. This variety of programs and the system of classification make it possible to fit a specific couple or family to a specific program.

PROGRAM LEADERSHIP

Marriage enrichment programs are led by people with varying backgrounds of professional status, degrees of training, and styles of leadership. Programs are conducted by: 1) nonprofessionally trained married couples working alone, trained for the particular program model they are leading (e.g., ACME: Hopkins et al., 1978); 2) married couples at least one of whom is a trained professional, and both are trained in the particular program model they are leading (e.g., Marriage Communications Lab: Smith and Smith, 1976); 3) nonprofessionally trained married couple, working together with a trained professional from one of the helping professions, trained in the particular model they are using (e.g., Marriage Encounter: Demarest et al., 1977); 4) male-female leadership team, but not necessarily married, trained in the particular model they are using (e.g., Relationship Enhancement Program: Guerney, 1977); and 5) an individual person, of either gender, trained in the particular model he or she is using (e.g., Couples Communication Program: Miller, Nunnally, and Wackman, 1975; Relationship Enhancement Program: Guerney, 1977).

Some programs permit a variety of the leadership options noted; others do not. The ACME model requires that leadership be provided by a married couple. In that model, leader teams often include at least one professional, but Mace and Mace suggest that lay couples may be just as effective (1976a). Mace (1975b) insists however that although an individual or unrelated male-female leadership team can lead an effective experience, the best facilitators for marriage enrichment weekend programs or marital growth groups are married couples who play a fully participative role and serve as models and even as surrogate parents. However, we are aware of no research which supports this position, though there is much in the way of subjective, personal testimony from leaders and participants which affirms it. Mace and Mace also suggest that clinically trained leaders should be available in at least a supervisory capacity for all marriage enrichment programs (1976a).

Couples Communication Program leaders are not required to be married couples or even male-female couples, though they may be (Miller, Nunnally, and Wackman, 1975). The Relationship Enhancement Program (Guerney, 1977) does not consider the use of individual leaders of either gender, as opposed to male-female teams, a severe handicap, and permits both possibilities. The Marriage Encounter program employs only married couples working with a trained professional (a clergyman). Malamud (1975) even uses leaderless groups for his program. Otto (1976) surveyed 30 professionals involved in marriage enrichment programming, and 90 percent reported they used either husband-wife or nonmarried, male-female leadership teams.

Leadership styles vary from nonparticipant, leader-director, to full participant-leader (Mace, 1975a). The Relationship Enhancement Program does not encourage the group leader to be a participant leader, that is, he is not encouraged to self-disclose or share personal moods, feelings, or reactions which arise as the group is led. On the other hand, leaders of the ACME model are full participants. Marriage Encounter leadership couples model self-disclosure of thoughts, feelings, and intentions, as well as risk-taking, vulnerability, and positive affirmation. Regardless of the style, most writers seem to agree that it is important for the leaders to model the skills they propose to teach and the growth-oriented relationship they value.

Use of Nonprofessionals and Paraprofessionals as Leaders

Most marriage enrichment programs permit and even encourage the use of appropriate nonprofessionals or paraprofessionals as leaders or facilitators (e.g., Guerney, 1977; L'Abate, 1977a; Hopkins et al., 1978; Regula, 1975). The research of Truax and Carkhuff (1967) has emphasized the therapeutic value of personality variables of the therapists, as opposed to formalized techniques. Empathy, warmth, and genuineness are identified as exerting a personal influence which contributes to successful outcomes (Goldstein, 1969). Truax and Carkhuff (1967) also demonstrate that training in empathy, warmth, and genuineness is possible. Goldstein (1969) refers to about 20 research reports which suggest or demonstrate the therapeutic potency of nurses, patient's parents, college undergraduates, psychological technicians, convicts, housewives, auxiliary counselors, human service aides, and foster grandparents. Collins (1977) and Guerney (1969) strongly suggest that nonprofessionals trained in empathy and appropriately supervised can be effective agents of change. All of this suggests that the use of appropriately trained and supervised nonprofessionals to facilitate growth with nonclinical, couple enrichment groups, and even with clinical couples or groups of couples (L'Abate, 1977a), is appropriate.

The use of nonprofessionals conceivably could lead to the dissemination of important growth-oriented services, at a reduced cost, to a larger portion of the population than would be reached if leadership were restricted to professionally trained persons. The use of nonprofessionals also conserves professional resources, allowing the professionals to serve as program developers, supervisors, and trainers of lay leadership (Guerney, 1977). If research further demonstrates that short-term marriage enrichment programs are as effective as claimed, then the economy of professional resources and cost, contributed to by the use of nonprofessional leadership, would argue even more strongly for this type of program to be used.

Leadership Training

Otto (1975, 1976) found that of the 30 professionals conducting enrichment programs he surveyed, over 80 percent were training other persons to lead programs as well. Most national marriage enrichment organizations have training guidelines and clearly defined standards for leaders. The need for highly qualified, trained leadership becomes evident when it is realized that the most important variable in the success of enrichment programs is identified as the quality of the leaders' skills and relationships (Lieberman, Yalom, and Miles, 1973; Mace and Mace, 1976b).

ACME (Hopkins et al., 1978) has developed standards for the selection, training, and certification of leaders of marriage enrichment programs. Many of the national marriage enrichment organizations have adopted these or similar standards. Selection standards include the following: 1) the couple are actively committed to marital growth; 2) the couple can work together, cooperatively as a team; 3) the couple can communicate in a warm and caring manner to other couples, and are sensitive to others in the group; 4) they are ready and able to openly share themselves and to be vulnerable; 5) they are aware of the group process and couple process occurring around them; and 6) they have some basic knowledge of human development, marital interaction, and group process.

ACME's training and certification standards include the following: 1) participation in a marriage enrichment event; 2) reflection on enrichment experiences regarding leadership and component parts of the program; 3) exposure to and discussion of a variety of styles, resources, and support systems for marriage enrichment; 4) practice in designing a marriage enrichment experience; 5) practice in leading a marriage enrichment experience; 6) marital exploration, or an intense marital dialogue, in front of other trainee couples; 7) reflection, evaluation, and development of an ongoing growth plan for themselves; 8) provisional certification by ACME; 9) participation in an advanced training workshop; 10) leadership of five marriage enrichment events, with evaluation from participants; 11) full certification for a three year period; and 12) a three-year review, with evidence of continuing marital growth and satisfactory couple group leadership needed for continuing certification.

Other leadership training programs differ somewhat from the ACME model. For example, the training programs of Guerney and L'Abate do not share ACME's emphasis on the leadership couple's active participation and sharing of themselves and their personal experiences within the program. In the Guerney and L'Abate programs, leaders serve as facilitators, not as co-participants; whereas, in the ACME model, both the facilitator and co-participant functions are equally emphasized. In addition to this difference, Guerney (1977, 1978) uses a more behaviorally oriented training approach which he suggests is applicable to a wide variety of programs. L'Abate advocates the use of detailed written instructions incorporated into training manuals, designed for many varied content areas (L'Abate and Collaborators, 1975).

In spite of this diversity in training models, training and certification of marriage enrichment leaders is becoming more specific and standardized. A combination of skill development, didactic learning, and actual supervised experiences as a leader appear to be common elements of all training programs. As the marriage enrichment movement grows, we can expect more attention to the training of competent leaders.

It is important that clinically trained professionals realize that their training as a marital or family therapist is not necessarily sufficient to qualify them as marriage enrichment program leaders. It is also important that enthusiastic nonprofessionals realize that having a growth-oriented, mutually satisfying marital relationship, and participation in a few marriage enrichment programs does not qualify them either to be effective program leaders.

PROGRAM COST

The cost of weekend experiences usually includes room and board, plus an amount pooled to provide a fee of from one hundred to three hundred dollars per leader couple. However, there are many leaders who receive no remuneration for their services, while others receive up to eight hundred dollars for leading a weekend program. (The latter is with clinical couples.) Likewise, the cost for professionally led multiweek programs ranges from one hundred to three hundred dollars. Other multiweek programs are cost-free. Either way, L'Abate (1977a) and Guerney (1977) have noted that enrichment, for the most part, is relatively inexpensive when compared to therapy, especially if the programs are led by trained nonprofessionals or paraprofessionals.

This brief overview of some of the available marriage enrichment programs demonstrates the varied designs, formats, techniques, and resources that are used. We have seen how programs vary with regard to time format, structure, and use of total group interaction, dyadic interaction, and interaction in small groups of several couples. The content areas which are focused on include: expressing wants, needs, expectations, feelings, and intentions; goals and values; communication skills; conflict-utilization skills; intimacy and affection; individual and marital strengths; negotiating marital roles; sexual fulfillment; parenting; and decision making and contracting. The list could go on endlessly. The extent to which these areas are emphasized differs considerably among programs. However, there is a variety of enrichment programs which focus specifically on one particular area, such as communication skills, the pre-marital relationship (e.g., Ginsberg & Vogelsong, 1977), effective parenting (e.g., DeRosis, 1970), and sexual enrichment for couples (e.g., Maddock, 1976; Lo Piccolo and Miller, 1978). Some marriage enrichment programs also offer a second or advanced experience beyond the basic weekend of multiweek experience (L'Abate, 1977a).

Programs also differ in the extent to which leaders are permitted and encouraged to change the format for each client group, even during a particular experience. For example, Marriage Enrichment, Inc. has no flexibility. However, Marriage Communication Lab has great flexibility and encourages its leaders and participants to develop their own program and be able to modify it according to the emerging needs of a particular group of couples. We need to note here that our value system requires that a clear theoretical rationale be present for all experiences in which clients are requested to participate.

Some couples may be intimidated by a psychologically oriented program and would rather choose one that is associated with a religious group. Conversely, other couples find the religious association contrary to their value system, and they choose not to participate in such programs.

The Association of Couples for Marriage Enrichment (ACME) affirms that all of the programs it recognizes, whatever the format, should meet the following guidelines: 1) the program should be led by one or more qualified married couples whose leadership reflects an ability to interact and participate effectively; 2) the program should be experiential and dynamic, as opposed to a didactic and purely intellectual program; 3) the program should provide an opportunity for couple dialogue and interaction in the total group as well as in private; 4) structured exercises should be used to facilitate dialogue or in response to it, to focus on specific issues or processes; 5) there should be a ratio of one leadership couple for each four to eight participant couples; 6) participant couples should have some voice in setting the agenda; and 7) program time should be at least fifteen hours, either in a weekend setting or in a series of sequential weekly meetings (Hopkins et al., 1978). Guidelines such as these may provide a base for ongoing discussion and research regarding the effectiveness of various program formats and designs.

To date, much of the appeal of marriage enrichment is to middle-class persons. The cognitive and theoretical emphasis, and the emphasis on verbal skills may limit the movement to middle-class and upper-class couples who value and comprehend the intellectual material. Even the cost and time involved in leaving the home environment for a weekend experience might be prohibitive for lower-class couples. Despite the fact that L'Abate (1977a) and Guerney (1977) insist that their models can be appropriately and effectively used with different socio-economic classes, applicability to other than middle-class and upper-class couples needs to be empirically verified.

Target Populations

Most marriage enrichment programming is aimed at nondysfunctional couples, and, in fact, many program leaders restrict participation in marriage enrichment programs to couples who are not in therapy. In this chapter, we challenge the common assumption that dysfunctional couples cannot benefit from the marriage enrichment process. A description of couples based on a continuum ranging from excellent marital relationship function to extreme marital relationship dysfunction is presented, and we suggest ways in which marriage enrichment, with appropriate modifications, can benefit couples at different points along this continuum.

In much of the marriage enrichment literature the assertion is made that programs are designed for and applicable to couples with a fairly well functioning relationship who want to make it better and not for couples with serious personal difficulties or troubled relationships (Clinebell, 1975; Hopkins and Hopkins, 1975; Hopkins et al, 1978; Koch and Koch, 1976; Mace and Mace, 1976a; Miller, 1975; Otto, 1976). It is apparent that programs which utilize leaders who are not clinically trained in marital therapy or counseling are not designed to cope with the potentially disruptive and destructive interactions of troubled couples. However, this does not mean that troubled couples could not or would not benefit from the program. It only indicates that the leadership, as presently viewed and trained, cannot manage these people and the disruptive aspects of their interactions, and that the program design is not arranged in such a way, or flexible enough, to be able to accommodate the dysfunctional interactions of couples who do not have a large core of marital health on which to build.

To make hard and fast distinctions between well-functioning marriages and troubled marriages is not as helpful as approaching the question of who can benefit from a marriage enrichment program from a continuum perspective.

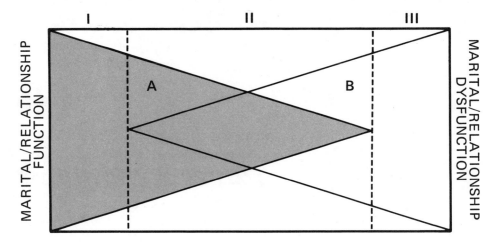

Figure 4.1. *Marital/Relationship Function/Dysfunction Continuum*

In Figure 4.1, Section I of the diagram represents functional couples deeply committed to a growth-oriented marital philosophy and to a disciplined involvement in the ongoing process of marriage enrichment. The relationship is characterized by a high degree of marital satisfaction, interdependent functioning, personal fulfillment, and a relatively high fulfillment of the potential of the relationship. There is a relative absence of intrapersonal or interpersonal dysfunction or pathology. We suggest that these couples would benefit *less* from involvement in a marriage enrichment program than would the couples in Section II. Section III of the diagram represents couples with deep-seated and pervasive intrapersonal or interpersonal pathology. At the far end of the continuum would be the psychotic person, the incipient psychotic, and the severely depressed person who could benefit little from such a program, if at all (Guerney, 1977). Relationships in this section are characterized by firmly entrenched problems, a high degree of disorganization, dysfunctional patterns of relating that have existed for a prolonged period of time, denial or externalization of problems, or uncooperative attitudes towards each other (L'Abate and Weeks, 1976). There is a relative absence of positive bonding and good will between the partners, and the relationship appears to be founded primarily upon neurotic needs, rather than mutual strengths or the desire to grow as individuals and as a couple. We suggest that these couples too would benefit *less* from involvement in a marriage enrichment program than would couples in Section II. The benefits for couples in Section III would be limited to diagnosis (L'Abate and Weeks, 1976), and possibly to the development of some specific skills which probably could not or would not be practiced in an integrated way within the current relationship because of the presence of the individual pathology or the dysfunctional patterns of relating.

Section II of the diagram represents couples on the continuum from (A) primarily well functioning relationships, with a relatively high degree of couple and individual satisfaction, and relatively minor problems, to (B) primarily dysfunctional relationships, with a relatively low degree of couple and individual satisfaction, and relatively major problems. This section includes those couples referred to as sub-clinical. That is, despite their love for each other and their commitment to the marriage, they are functioning below optimum level and need help with their problems (Otto, 1976). We suggest that these couples could benefit more from involvement in a marriage enrichment program than would couples in Sections I or III. It is hoped that those closer to the dysfunctional end of the continuum will be able to discover their dysfunctional patterns and learn how to relate more effectively before their problems become seriously entrenched pathological symptoms (Wright and L'Abate, 1977). At the least, these couples might recognize that they need more help than the program can offer and will thus seek a referral to appropriate counseling or therapy (Dixon and Sciara, 1977).

With a continuum perspective, it becomes not a question of who can or cannot benefit from the marriage enrichment experience, but a questions of which particular program is best for which particular couple. What type of structure and leadership style would best benefit this couple at their level of development?

For example, in a limited study, Neville (1971) suggests that there is a differential response among various personality types to marriage enrichment group experiences, and that such groups are more familiar and complementary to some personality types than others. He concluded that intuitive-feeling-perceptive personality types found their experience *in that particular type of program* (a marital encounter group) to merge with their lifestyle and were at ease with the process. Although sensing-thinking-judging personality types may have been uncomfortable with some aspects of the process, the results indicated that they responded well to the experience, perhaps because they had thoughtfully analyzed the experience, concluded it was a logical and sensible approach, and had thus committed themselves to the process. Further research on other programs might provide the means to fit an individual with a particular personality type to a particular program. They could be matched in such a way that sufficient cognitive and affective dissonance could be developed for learning and change to take place. At the same time, the match would also be made in such a way that the program would not be so radically alien to the personality type of the participant as to produce so much anxiety or resistance that he would be prevented from accepting the experience and deriving benefit from it.

Another example develops this point further. The Marriage Encounter experience (Bosco, 1972; Demarest et al., 1977; Genovese, 1975) is an intense, highly structured, weekend experience, with the focus almost entirely upon the interaction of each couple (as opposed to a group of couples). A specific kind of couple dialogue is practiced throughout the weekend. The leadership team makes several presentations to the total group. Then, in the privacy of their own room, each couple reflects upon what has been said, and answers questions related to the presentation, recording them in a notebook. The written self-disclosure is then shared between partners in complete privacy from the others. After each has read the other's self-disclosure, each partner encourages the other to verbally develop and further describe the written feelings, in an attempt to experience each other more fully at an affective level.

Huber (Note 3) has made an attempt to evaluate the Marriage Encounter weekend experience. Although his research suffers from several shortcomings (Gurman and Kniskern, 1977), notably the limitation of relying on participant self-evaluation and the lack of long-term follow-up, his findings may still have value. Experimental group husbands, in comparison to control group husbands, were found to score significantly higher on four major Caring Relationship Inventory (Shostrom, 1967) scales: Affection, Friendship, Eros, and Empathy. Females in the experimental group showed no significant change when compared to females in the control group on any of the major scales. Overall positive changes lasted for at least six weeks.

Such results raise some interesting questions. For example, why are males affected in these areas, and not females? Is it possible that the high degree of structure, the rule and norm of self-disclosure, the extreme privacy, and the perception that the experience is logical and sensible (Neville, 1971), interact to provide a safe atmosphere and an environment conducive to change for certain males? Many males are culturally scripted to think logically, to work hard in a disciplined and even compulsive manner, and to be nondemonstrative and nonexpressive with their feelings (Balswick and Peck, 1971). The Marriage Encounter experience may provide the necessary atmosphere and environment for some of the males described above to break the cultural script regarding self-disclosure and affective expression by following the rules of the Encounter experience.

If effective research could demonstrate that these, or other similar hypotheses, are correct, then the implications for referral to such a program would be obvious. Such a program might be suggested for a relatively well functioning couple in which it was perceived that the husband (and the relationship) could benefit most directly from experiencing and expressing his feelings and other appropriate self-disclosures. The wife would presumably benefit from the increased friendship, empathy, and so forth from her partner. On the other hand, this program might not be suggested for a couple who already have the ability to share on a significantly affective level with each other, but who need to learn specific skills in areas such as conflict resolution or problem solving. Nor, would this program be suggested for a couple on the dysfunctional end of the continuum, where the need for monitoring the couple's interaction is greater than that provided for in the structure of the Marriage Encounter program.

Though much of this is only conjectural at this point, we believe it deserves mention. If marriage enrichment programs are effective we need to know with more clarity which particular program, structure, and leadership style would benefit which particular couples. It is hoped the time will come when enrichment programs can be matched to the intrapersonal and interpersonal needs of the couple, and to the socioeconomic, and educational levels of the couple (Guerney, 1977; L'Abate, 1974; L'Abate and Collaborators, 1975).

We have concluded from our own experience and review of many of the currently available programs that the greater the amount of relationship dysfunction, the greater the need for the following: 1) a high degree of structure; 2) a limited and well-focused agenda; 3) highly skilled and active leadership trained in marital and individual therapy and group dynamics; 4) some conjoint crisis-intervention therapy during the experience, or branching, which is the use of structured mini-programs to deal with emerging issues tangential to the enrichment process (L'Abate, 1977a); 5) close attention to screening (Guerney, 1977; L'Abate, 1977a; Liberman et al., 1976; Smith and Alexander, 1974); and 6) smaller group size (five to six couples).

The greater the amount of relationship function, the less need there is for these six factors to be present in the program. This is not to imply that a thoughtfully designed program, with clear goals and specific objectives, and appropriately trained and skilled leadership, is not needed at the more functional end of the continuum. They most certainly are. Nor, is it to imply that couples at that end of the continuum could not benefit from a highly structured, limited-agenda program, with highly skilled leaders trained in marriage and individual therapy and group dynamics. They most certainly can. But, with programs developed for these couples, there is also the possibility for greater flexibility with structure; a more varied agenda; less forced and repeated skill practice (because couples can and will practice on their own); less close monitoring of the interactions of participants; greater use of small, leaderless, sharing groups, composed of participant couples; and a greater reliance upon peer leadership which has been appropriately prepared and trained in the design and leadership of marriage enrichment programs.

None of these suggestions have been empirically researched to this point. Our personal experience with the use of identical marriage enrichment programs with groups of well-functioning couples and groups of troubled couples in ongoing therapy, varying only our leadership style, leads us to hypothesize that such research would probably support many of the suggestions. Research is sorely needed, and could possibly lead to the extension of the benefits of marriage enrichment to a broader section of the population than is currently envisioned.

The specific benefits that the more dysfunctional couples might obtain from participation in a marriage enrichment program will, of course, vary depending upon the couple and the program. To illustrate the types of benefits that are possible for these couples, we will present brief case examples for two couples who participated in a Creative Marriage Enrichment weekend during the course of conjoint marital therapy.

Case 1. Bob and Sally, a couple in their mid-twenties, who had been married for four years, sought marital therapy after a brief separation. At the time of therapy intake, Bob was convinced that he had to end the marriage in order to be happy. Sally was confused and hurt, believing that Bob's dissatisfaction and desire to leave had come without warning. The couple described their relationship as one in which Bob tended to be noncommunicative and to withdraw at any sign of conflict, while Sally was frequently critical and nagging.

After nine weeks of therapy, the couple was interacting in a more satisfying, although still dysfunctional, way. Bob was less depressed and had started communicating more. As the couple's communication improved, Sally found that she was being less critical. In fact, there had been such a marked improvement in the marital interaction, that the couple was considering terminating therapy to save money. At this point, the therapist recommended the marriage enrichment weekend as an opportunity for Bob and Sally to learn more about communication techniques and to share their positive feelings and thoughts.

Prior to the marriage enrichment weekend, Sally had been afraid to hear what Bob had been keeping to himself. Provoked by her prodding, he had come out of his detachment a few times before and had bitterly chastised her. The enrichment weekend helped Bob to learn that communicating one's feelings is not automatically destructive. Also, for the first time, Bob experienced conflict resolution as cooperation, rather than combat, a totally new concept for him. The experiences which focused on the exchange of positive statements reassured Sally that Bob was at least capable of learning how to give the emotional support and warmth she had been craving and demanding. Most importantly perhaps, the marriage enrichment program helped the couple to see the difference between the level that they had already reached by decreasing the number of strained silences and angry outbursts, and the level of companionship and cooperation that they *could* reach through improved communication and individual functioning.

After several additional months of marital therapy, the couple had attained a much more satisfying and functional relationship.

Case 2. Norman and Joan had been married for 13 years when they began therapy. They had been in marital therapy two years earlier, but quit when they felt that little progress was being made. They worked on and resolved a number of relationship issues and, two months prior to the marriage enrichment weekend, they contracted to work in sex therapy. They were referred to the marital enrichment weekend in part because their progress in sensate focus/pleasuring exercises had been hampered by their inability to candidly discuss their pleasuring likes and dislikes with each other.

After participation in the marriage enrichment weekend, Joan began to feel that sexual pleasuring with her husband was not selfish after all. Moreover, she learned that she could communicate to Norman that she was not interested in sex without making him feel rejected as a person. Norman, in turn, learned not to hold back his angry feelings. He was impressed that fighting fair was an option he had not heard of before the weekend.

During an exercise in which each couple held hands and then let go in order to experience being alone, Joan became quite upset, and was surprised that she had difficulty standing alone. Since she had frequently accused her husband of being overdependent, this experience of her own dependency needs was particularly salient to her and increased her tolerance of his needs.

Several of the exercises reminded Joan of shortcomings that she had. Listing her feelings about herself was an exercise she found discouraging because of the many things she felt she wanted to change. Her dissatisfaction with herself was, however, counterbalanced by her joy in being able to share some of her feelings with Norman for the first time.

Norman and Joan continued in couple therapy for ten months, and they made substantial progress in overcoming their relationship problems and in improving their sexual relationship.

In neither of these case illustrations do we believe that the marriage enrichment weekend helped the couples to identify or to solve problems that they would otherwise have missed in therapy. Rather, we believe that the marriage enrichment program helped them to focus more clearly on the problems much sooner than they would have. More importantly, the enrichment experience seemed to have led to a new, positive feeling towards each other and the marital relationship and a mutual commitment to work on long-standing problems.

We do not view marriage enrichment programs as a substitute for ongoing marital or relationship therapy for dysfunctional couples. However, Guerney (1977) does see the Relationship Enhancement Program as an appropriate treatment program for certain relationship difficulties. Also, Clinebell (1975) refers to "growth counseling" as a human potential approach to counseling and enrichment, focusing on enriching ordinary marriages and on helping couples in crisis to view and use their conflicts as opportunities for growth. It involves a movement away from a remedial-corrective and sickness-diagnosis-treatment model towards a health-prevention, potential-development growth model. There is a distinct emphasis on the positive and the creative possibilities of the relationship. Such counseling is action oriented, aimed at providing a supportive relationship, helping with problem analysis, and taking immediate action steps. It is short-term and is claimed to be effective with couples who are still committed to the marital relationship and are willing to work together to enhance the relationship. For more deeply troubled couples, traditional marital therapy is deemed appropriate.

Wright and L'Abate (1977) (referring to families in particular) view therapy, enrichment, education and behavior modification as four, overlapping, valuable, approaches, used separately, or in selective combination, to facilitate effective family and marital functioning. They argue that none of the four is to be seen as primary. Rather, each is viewed as having a valuable and appropriate role to play in family or marital facilitation, and personal preference or prejudice should not be the criteria for employing or not employing a particular method or approach. They call for appropriate research of this multi-modal approach and appropriate training in the theory and practice of all four approaches.

We think this view clearly shows that at times, the boundaries between enrichment, education, and therapy are not always very clear. Marriage enrichment programming can be preventive, enriching, and therapeutic, depending upon the program's goals and objectives, when it is undertaken, the length of the program, and the orientation or perspective of the participants and the leaders (Guerney, 1977; L'Abate, 1977a). Guerney (1977) has qustioned the need to differentiate between therapy, prevention, and enrichment, when such distinctions have been rather arbitrary to date and have not been based upon thorough comparative research. The issue deserves more careful attention and research, but for the time being, we assume that many practitioners will continue to make the differentiation.

To those who do differentiate between marriage enrichment and therapy, marriage enrichment programs may be viewed primarily as an important and beneficial adjunct to marital and relationship therapy for dysfunctional couples (Clinebell, 1975; Guerney, 1977; L'Abate 1977a; Wright and L'Abate, 1977). The specific skill training that is a part of many marriage enrichment programs can be very helpful to clients in treatment and aid in their progress. For example, in their group counseling, Smith and Alexander (1974) use a variety of enrichment or growth-oriented experiences and group and couple cohesiveness-enhancing experiences to expand the focus of the couple and group beyond couple problems. They attempt to broaden the focus to include strengths and actual experiences of closeness and caring, even within a period of stress in the marital relationship. L'Abate (1977a) sometimes employs enrichment programming for an individual couple or family unit, as opposed to the usual use with groups of couples or families.

Of course, as noted above, careful screening is needed for client couples in stressed situations before participation in a marriage enrichment program is suggested. It is conceivable that as many as three or more sessions could be used for evaluation, problem identification, ventilation and abreaction of feelings, and goal setting. Such a procedure would permit the reduction of negative feelings which could block the couple's participation in a postively-oriented program. It would also permit the establishment of a therapeutic alliance which could serve as an empathic and concerned model for the couple and a relationship to which they could return for further counseling after the marriage enrichment experience is over (Liberman et al., 1976). At the Marriage Council of Philadelphia, we suggest that our therapists use the following screening guidelines for couples in therapy before referring them to our Marriage Enrichment Program (M.E.P.). The program is for *our clients only* at the present time. The screening guidelines are the following:

1) The program is for couples in ongoing therapy having completed at least three to eight sessions.

2) Therapeutic alliances between clients and therapists already must be established.

3) Therapists must sense that the couple could benefit from such a growth enrichment program. (i.e., This program is not to be used when all else has failed!)

4) The couple must demonstrate a willingness to return to therapy following the M.E.P.

5) There must be a reasonable amount of good will between the partners. (That is, there should be some degree of positive bonding and commitment to work on improving the relationship in a group setting.)

We encourage therapists to speak directly to the program coordinator regarding the advisability of placing a particular couple in this program (Hof, Note 4).

Marriage enrichment programming can be employed concurrently with the beginning, middle, or ending phases of therapy (Guerney, 1977; L'Abate, 1977a; Wright and L'Abate, 1977), or subsequent to therapy (Guerney, 1977). In these instances, it would be seen as having a remedial, secondary, or tertiary preventive function.

Most couples in therapy are there because they are in pain and want relief. They are frequently survival-oriented and involved in a closed system which is not conducive to growth. (Of course, many couples not involved in therapy are in the same position.) Frequently the therapist must first help the couple to lower defenses, to develop a sense of who they are, and to build new relationship skills, before they can become oriented to a growth model and benefit significantly from marriage enrichment experiences.

In the beginning of therapy, if hostility is not too pervasive, participation in a marriage enrichment program can serve a diagnostic function. Participation at this point can also help to identify and highlight specific strengths which could then be utilized and expanded as therapy progresses. In the middle or later phases of therapy, such participation could enable the couple to develop, practice, and integrate specific, needed skills in areas such as communication, empathy, and conflict utilization. It could also lead to the development of a deeper level of positive feeling towards each other and of the potential of the relationship. In a group setting, growth can be reinforced, peer support and feedback can be received, and couples can help other couples to grow. Participation in an ongoing marital growth group with other nonclinical couples, towards the end of therapy and beyond, could serve as a half-way house for previously dysfunctional couples. This could enable them to receive and give support, to be involved in a continuing growth experience in which they could integrate their learning and develop their potential as a couple, working along with other couples (Clinebell, 1975).

It needs to be clearly stated that some marriages are not conducive to personal growth and enrichment, and are, in fact, destructive. For these relationships, divorce can be seen as a growth step, and many proponents of marriage enrichment clearly affirm this position. Marriage enrichment experiences are viewed as potentially helping troubled couples find help sooner, as adjunctive to ongoing therapy, and as helping destructive relationships to end sooner (Clinebell, 1975). Drawing on his own use of marriage enrichment programs with clinical couples, David Mace has suggested that the focus on the couple's primary coping system and the positive emphasis sometimes result in major relationship changes, even obviating the need to deal with the pathological aspects of the relationship. In fact, he claims that in some cases, the pathology seems to wither away (Note 5). Needless to say, if research supports these suggestions and the experiences of Mace and others, the implications for the field of marital and relationship therapy are profound.

ᴥ 5

Research on Marriage Enrichment

In this, the final chapter of Section I, we turn our attention to the research literature on marriage enrichment. Our review of this literature confirms our belief that the research on marital enrichment programs is still in its infancy. When viewed within the context of the large number of couples who have been participants in these programs, the amount of research seems very small. In this chapter, we examine the reasons for the limited research in this field, briefly discuss the methodological problems of marital enrichment research, critically evaluate the published studies, and suggest directions for future research.

There is a scarcity of research in the marital enrichment field. This is due, in part, to the difficulty of evaluating the effectiveness of marital enrichment programs. Outcome research on marriage enrichment shares the numerous scientific, ethical, and practical problems encountered with the measurement of outcome of other psychological change processes. For example, researchers must insure that the treatments are precisely specified, that changes are not due to the characteristics of the particular therapists involved, and that factors such as passage of time and placebo effects are adequately controlled. Added to these common problems, however, is a methodological difficulty that is particularly troublesome for conducting research on marriage enrichment: selection of appropriate measures of change.

The problem of selecting outcome measures for marital enrichment programs stems from two sources. First, almost all psychological outcome research has been done with therapy programs in clinical settings, and, therefore, the outcome measures that have been used focus on elimination of symptoms or problematic interactions. The emphasis of marriage enrichment programs, however, has been on improving and enhancing the relationships of nonclinical couples. Effective research on the outcome of marriage enrichment experiences will depend partially on the development of measures that can assess improvements in couples' relating from the satisfactory to the more-than-satisfactory level.

The second source of this measurement problem is the unfortunate tendency of many to describe the goals of marriage enrichment in such a global and undifferentiated manner, that it is extremely difficult to specify the types of changes that are expected, or to derive an operational definition for the changes desired. A researcher is in a very difficult position if he must try to demonstrate through quantitative measures that a couple has, for example, "increased the creative potential for their relationship."

The difficulty of conducting the research is, however, only one factor contributing to the scarcity of research on marriage enrichment. Perhaps the most important factor is that so many programs are led by or created by nonprofessionals, people with little training or interest in research. Those not trained in experimental methods may understandably view research as a mysterious and difficult endeavor. This viewpoint need not stand in the way of conducting research on marriage enrichment, however, since program leaders with a commitment to empirical validation of their techniques could open their programs to study by researchers. What does interfere with such collaborative efforts, and what is most troubling to us, is the negative attitude toward research and researchers among many nonprofessionals and even some professionals and the too common perception of research as artificial and unnecessary.

The negative attitude towards research and researchers, among many in the marriage enrichment field, may be due largely to fears and misconceptions about research. There is the belief that the scrutinizing, measuring, and quantifying involved in research violates the humanistic tradition of marriage enrichment and reflects the researchers' lack of concern for the whole person and the whole relationship. Furthermore, there is the fear that the researcher's scientific skepticism and "I need proof" approach represent a desire to tear down the hard work of marriage enrichment program developers and to portray the programs as worthless and ineffective. Of all people, however, workers in the field of marriage enrichment should understand that hostility and negative attitudes often arise not from real differences in values and beliefs, but from inadequate communication about needs and perceptions.

Researchers need to be attuned to these fears and misconceptions if they hope to ever be permitted to conduct extensive research on the variety of marriage enrichment programs. Rather than presenting themselves as the discerners of the real truth, researchers need to stress the positive benefits that can result from their work, that is, to validate, refine, and to better understand the process and outcome of marriage enrichment. In addition, while a scientific skepticism toward the enthusiastic claims of marriage enrichment leaders and participants is necessary for the researcher, he need not treat those claims with hostility or derision. The appropriate scientific attitude is one of neutrality. Finally, researchers must recognize and accept the fact that the difficulty of assessing the outcome of marriage enrichment is due not only to the program developers' failures at operationalizing goals, but also to the researchers' failures to design and validate appropriate outcome measures. In particular, measures of marital and individual health and adjustment, as opposed to pathology and maladjustment, need to be developed.

In order to evaluate the outcome of marriage enrichment programs, the researchers must study and evaluate only components of the programs, focusing on the observable and quantifiable parts, giving less attention and credence to subjective self-report. Leaders of marriage enrichment programs need to know and understand that these actions are dictated by the nature of the experimental method and do not reflect a rejection on the part of the researchers of either the importance of seeing the program as an integrated whole or the importance of the subjective responses of the participants. Subjective responses are not sufficient for the *scientific* demonstration of the effectiveness of marriage enrichment programs. Good science requires that the outcome of a marriage enrichment experience be publicly verifiable and replicable, and, therefore, measurable. Thus, creators of marriage enrichment programs need to be much more specific and concrete in describing the types of individual and relationship changes that they are trying to produce.

It is only through careful empirical research with appropriate controls and assessment of outcome with reliable and valid measurement techniques that we can learn whether marriage enrichment programs achieve their stated goals. The participants and leaders of any educational or therapeutic change process cannot know whether changes in their subjective feeling states, perceptions, attitudes, or behaviors are a consequence of the specific technique employed or of nonspecific effects of participation (e.g., expectancy factors, contact with a therapist or leader, contact with other participants, suggestion, or demand factors). Nor can those involved in a change process know with any certainty to what extent similar changes might have occurred simply with the passage of time.

Research on marriage enrichment also would allow us to identify the specific types of changes and the stability of changes over a period of time that are associated with participation in the program. We can, through research, directly compare the effectiveness of two or more different programs and identify those components of the programs that are the active ingredients. Finally, research can answer questions about the suitability of various programs for people with varying degrees and types of problems, personality styles and traits, and social and demographic characteristics.

Of course, in order for research to provide us with the answers we need, the research itself must meet certain scientific criteria. It is not our purpose to provide here a detailed treatment of experimental design and analysis of data. We do need, however, to suggest certain guidelines that the reader can use for evaluating the quality of research and to highlight certain methodological issues particularly relevant to research on marriage enrichment. What follows is a listing of the most important criteria for evaluating research on the effectiveness of marriage enrichment programs.

RANDOMIZATION

When couples are assigned to two or more experimental conditions, for example, a group of couples participating in a marriage enrichment program and a group of couples in a waiting list control group, assignment of the couples to one group or another should be done randomly. Without such random assignment, we cannot know whether differences between groups at the end of the program are due to the differences in the experimental conditions or to differences between the couples in the different groups that were present at the start.

CONTROL GROUPS

Any of a number of control groups may be used, but at the minimum, a waiting list control or a no treatment control group is necessary. These control groups allow us to separate changes that may occur as a result of the marriage enrichment experience from those changes that are due to the passage of time and effects of ongoing life experiences.

Beyond this basic requirement, other comparison groups can be useful. For example, an attention-placebo control group, which involves assignment of a group of couples to a treatment condition believed to be therapeutically or educationally inert, permits the assessment of the degree of change caused by nonspecific treatment factors such as expectancy for change or suggestion.

Another experimental design would entail assigning couples to two or more experimental treatments of different enrichment programs. A waiting list or no treatment control group would still be needed, however, since demonstration of the superiority of one program over another does not tell us how changes that may occur with either program compare to changes that result spontaneously with the passage of time.

MEASUREMENT CONSIDERATIONS

The way in which change is actually measured should be influenced by several factors. The measurement process is a major concern in outcome research, since no amount of elegance in experimental design or statistical analysis of data can overcome the use of poorly selected measurement tools. The following factors need to be considered when evaluating measurement techniques:

Timing of measurement. The most commonly encountered design in marital enrichment research involves measurements a short time before (pre) and a short time after (post) the enrichment experience and at a comparable time interval for the waiting list control group. There must be, however, provision for testing at yet another time, as a follow-up to the enrichment program. Without follow-up evaluation, we have no way of knowing whether changes that are seen at post-testing persist for any length of time after participation in the enrichment exprience has ended. At the least, the time between post-testing and follow-up should be one month.

Use of multiple outcome measures. Assessments of feelings, attitudes, beliefs, and behaviors can be made in a variety of ways. The participants and leaders can provide their own self-reports, and such self-reports can be obtained through structured or unstructured tests, questionnaires, or interviews. Observational measures may be obtained by independent judges or raters either in an experimentally controlled situation or in the naturalistic setting.

No one measurement technique is inherently better than another. The two major types of measurements, self-report and observation, both have their strengths and weaknesses. Reliance on only one measurement technique necessarily will exclude some important information needed to evaluate outcome.

Reliability and validity of measurement devices. Reliability of measurement refers to the degree to which multiple measurements with the same instrument or procedure produce similar scores. The validity of a measurement device refers to the extent to which the device measures what it purports to measure. Any study on the effectiveness of marriage enrichment should employ measurement devices of known reliability and validity or should seek to demonstrate the reliability and validity of the measures as part of the study. Relying solely on home made tests and questionnaires of unknown reliability or validity throws into question the meaning of the results.

This discussion highlights the major methodological issues that must be considered when evaluating research on the effectiveness of marriage enrichment programs. Let us now turn to an examination of the existing research literature on marriage enrichment. This examination will address two questions: do the available studies of marriage enrichment meet the methodological criteria for good research? and what qustions do the existing studies answer, or raise?

Before considering these questions, we must note that reviewing the research literature is made difficult by the lack of a generally accepted definition of marriage enrichment, and the fact that different clinicians and researchers have defined the term in a variety of ways. It is difficult to determine whether a paticular study should be included or excluded from a review of research on enrichment. For example, Beck (1975) classified only five of the outcome studies of marital counseling she reviewed as studies of marriage enrichment. Yet, many of the 29 studies Gurman and Kniskern (1977) included in their review of marriage enrichment programs can be found in Beck's article, but listed by Beck as studies of marital counseling or communication training.

For the present review, we have included studies of couples who have participated in programs that either have been clearly identified by the investigators as marital enrichment programs or consist of procedures and techniques that are major programmatic elements of marriage enrichment programs. We have included, therefore, not only studies of programs such as Marriage Encounter (Huber, Note 3) and the Pairing Enrichment Program (Travis and Travis, 1976a), but also research on such closely related programs as the Couples Communication Program (Miller et al., 1976b) and the Conjugal Relationship Enhancement Program (Guerney, 1977). The originators of the latter programs have clearly associated them with marriage enrichment and have been affiliated with marriage enrichment organizations such as the Council of Affiliated Marriage Enrichment Organizations (CAMEO) (Hopkins et al., 1978). Finally, a number of reports on other communication training and behavioral exchange procedures have been included in the research review. Although some of these studies do not purport to be assessments of marriage enrichment, the training techniques employed are similar or identical to the main programmatic elements of many marriage enrichment programs.

Thus, the programs studied differ markedly in their definition of marital enrichment, format, goals, and scope. These programmatic differences, as well as differences in research methodology, and in the type of dependent measures used, make it difficult to draw general conclusions from the studies reviewed.

With few exceptions, research on the outcome of marital enrichment experiences has involved a pre-post assessment format with two groups, the treatment group and a waiting-list or no-treatment control group. Due to this similarity in research design, we have decided not to present a detailed examination of each study. Rather, our intention is to summarize what is and is not currently known about the effectiveness of marital enrichment. The reader who is interested in the specific details of any of the studies reviewed is referred to the original reports and to Table 1.

Table 1 presents some basic information about 40 different studies of marital enrichment. (There are 42 listings in the table, but two studies are referenced under each of two different program formats.) As mentioned earlier, marital enrichment programs vary considerably in format and structure. In order to facilitate comparisons between studies, we have identified three general types of marital enrichment programs: those which focus primarily on communication training; those based mainly on behavioral exchange principles; and those programs which offer a varied mix of experiences and exercises. The various outcome measures used have been separated into the three categories suggested by Gurman and Kniskern (1977): overall marital adjustment; perceptual and individual personality variables, such as, perception of spouse, self-esteem and self-actualization; and relationship skill variables, such as communication and problem-solving skills, self-disclosure, and empathy.

The most basic question to be addressed by outcome research is whether the intervention procedure is followed by specific affective, attitudinal, cognitive, or behavioral changes. As Table 1 shows, most of the outcome studies reviewed do report positive changes on at least some measures following a marital enrichment experience. Furthermore, significant changes are not restricted to any particular type or class of variables.

Are the changes that follow participation in marital enrichment programs a result of the enrichment experience, the passage of time, or non-specific, that is, placebo, effects? Table 1 shows that 33 of the 40 studies (82.5%) used either a waiting-list or no-treatment control group. Since the general finding for these studies is that significantly greater change occurs for the marital enrichment group than for the control group, we can view the changes that occur as being due to factors other than the simple passage of time.

Table 1 also indicates that only one study used an attention-placebo control group. Roberts (1975) formed a placebo condition by placing five couples in an unstructured group setting in which issues could be discussed, but where the various enrichment experiences and exercises were not present. This placebo condition controlled for changes that might occur as a result of group participation and discussion in the absence of the specific enrichment experiences. Roberts (1975) reported that greater changes did occur in the placebo group than in a waiting-list control group. The marital enrichment group was, however, superior to both control groups. Thus, although non-specific treatment factors did produce positive changes, the enrichment experience itself resulted in greater changes.

Dixon and Sciara (1977) attempted to demonstrate a causal relationship between treatment intervention and changes in self-ratings of the relationship through use of a multiple baseline procedure, rather than a placebo control group. Their results suggest that changes in ratings are contingent upon the introduction of specific, reciprocity-exchange procedures.

Table 1. Outcome Research of Marriage Enrichment Experiences.

Author	Control groups[a]			Outcome measures[b]			Follow-up	Results[c]
	WL/NT	Pl.	AT.	Class	Self-report	Independent ratings		
Mixed Experiences/Exercises								
Bruder (1972)	Y	N	N	MA,P,RS	Y	N	N	P = +; MA,RS = −
Burns (1972)	Y	N	N	P	Y	N	Y	±
Huber (Note 3) (Marriage Encounter)	Y	N	N	P	Y	N	Y	Mostly +
Kilmann, Moreault, and Robinson (1978)	Y	N	Y	MA,P	Y	N	Y	+
Kilmann, Julian, and Moreault (1978)	Y	N	Y	MA,P,RS	Y	Y	N	+
L'Abate (1977a)	Y	N	N	P	Y	N	N	+
Swicegood (1974) (ACME)	Y	N	N	P,RS	Y	Y	Y	Mostly +
Travis and Travis (1976a) (Pairing Enrichment Program)	Y	N	N	P	Y	N	N	Mostly −
Travis and Travis (1976b)	N	N	N	P	Y	N	N	+
Weinstein (1975)	Y	N	N	P	Y	N	N	+
Communication Training								
Minnesota Couples Communication Program								
Beaver (1978)	Y	Y	N	RS	Y	N	N	±
Brown (1976)	Y	Y	N	P	Y	N	N	+
Campbell (1974)	Y	N	N	RS	N	Y	N	+
Dillon (1975)	Y	N	N	MA,P,RS	Y	N	Y	+
Larsen (1974)	N	N	N	P,RS	Y	N	N	±
Miller (1971)	Y	N	N	P,RS	Y	Y	N	P = ±, RS = +
Nunnally (1971)	Y	N	N	RS	Y	Y	N	Mostly +
Schwager and Conrad (1974)	N	N	N	P	Y	N	N	+
Thielen, Hubner, and Schmook (1976)	Y	N	Y	MA,P,RS	Y	Y	N	Mostly +
Witkin (Note 6)	Y	N	N	MA,RS	Y	Y	Y	±

Conjugal Relationship Enhancement Program

Study			Measures[b]			Outcome[c]
Collins (1971)	Y	Y	MA,RS	N	N	±
D'Augelli, Deyss, Guerney, Hershenberg, and Sborofsky (1974)	Y	N	RS	Y	N	+
Ely, Guerney, and Stover (1973)	Y	Y	RS	Y	N	±
Rappaport (1976)	Y	Y	MA,P,RS	N	N	+
Schlien (1971)	Y	Y	P,RS	Y	N	Mostly +
Wieman (1973)[d]	Y	Y	MA,RS	Y	Y	+

Other Communication Training

Study			Measures[b]			Outcome[c]
Epstein and Jackson (1978)	Y	Y	RS	Y	N	Mostly +
Hines (1976)	Y	N	RS	Y	N	+
Nadeau (1971)	Y	Y	P,RS	Y	Y	±
Neville (1971)	N	Y	P,RS	N	N	+
Orling (1976)	Y	Y	MA,P	N	N	+
Pilder (1972)	Y	Y	P,RS	Y	N	±
Van Zoost (1973)	N	Y	P,RS	Y	N	±
Venema (1976)[d]	N	Y	MA,P,RS	N	N	Mostly +
Williams (1975)	Y	Y	MA,RS	N	N	–

Behavior Exchange

Study			Measures[b]			Outcome[c]
Dixon and Sciara (1977)	N	Y	P,RS	N	N	Mostly +
Fisher (1973)	Y	Y	P	N	N	Mostly +
Harrell and Guerney (1976)	Y	Y	MA,P,RS	Y	Y	RS = ±; MA,P = –
McIntosh (1975)	Y	Y	MA,P,RS	N	N	–
Roberts (1975)	Y	Y	MA,P	N	N	+
Venema (1976)[d]	N	Y	MA,P,RS	N	N	Mostly –
Wieman (1973)[d]	Y	Y	MA,RS	Y	Y	+

Note: Y = Yes, N = No

[a] WL/NT = Waiting-List or No-Treatment Group; Pl. = Placebo-Control Group; A.T. = Alternate Therapy, i.e., the experimental group is compared with another therapy or enrichment group.

[b] Outcome measures are divided into three classes or groups; MA = measures of marital adjustment, P = perceptual and personality measures, RS = relationship-skill measures. Measures may also be based on self-report or ratings by independent observers or judges.

[c] + = statistically significant pre-post change and, when used, greater change than control group; ± = mixed results; – = negative results.

[d] Two studies, Venema (1976) and Wieman (1973), are listed twice, since each study can be grouped under two different categories of enrichment.

It is unfortunate that only two of the studies reviewed included some type of control for placebo effects. Such a group is particularly necessary, because, as Roberts (1975) demonstrated, nonspecific treatment factors can lead to significant changes in self-reported marital adjustment and in relationships. This finding raises the obvious question of whether some of the significant changes reported in the other studies reviewed here are due to so called placebo effects, and not to the marital enrichment experience itself.

Are the measurements made with reliable and valid instruments and are independent ratings, as well as self-report measures, used? Only 16 of the 40 studies (40%) have included independent raters or judges, whereas 37 of the studies (92.5%) have used self-report measures. Although self-report is more economical and convenient to obtain than ratings of objective observers, there are serious dangers in relying exclusively on measures that are so easily influenced by response biases, social desirability, and demand characteristics. Another drawback to the studies which have used only self-report as a measure of outcome is that often the instruments used are of unknown reliability and validity.

Do the reported outcomes represent stable or temporary changes in the participants? Eight of the forty studies (20%) included some type of follow-up assessment. Burns (1972) and Huber (Note 3) reported maintenance of changes in self-perception and perception of spouse, respectively, from post-test to follow-up, and Wieman (1973) found that changes in marital adjustment, expressive and responsive skill, and specific target behaviors were stable over a ten-week follow-up period. In addition, Dillon (1975) obtained significant changes in self-reported communication, self-esteem, and marital satisfaction that were maintained over ten weeks. Nadeau (1971), Swicegood (1974), and Witkin (Note 6) also reported some stability in changes following marital enrichment experiences. However, in Nadeau's study, self-report changes were better maintained than behavioral changes, while in Witkin's study behavioral, but not self-report, measures changed significantly with gains being maintained for a two month follow-up period. In Swicegood, some of the changes in perception of the relationship, marital integration, and communication were not maintained at follow-up. Kilmann, Moreault, and Robinson (1978) also found that some changes were maintained at follow-up, while others were not. In addition, significant improvement did not emerge for some variables until follow-up testing. Although the results of follow-up are for the most part encouraging, more studies need to be done with follow-up measures before we can conclude that marital enrichment does lead to stable changes in relationships.

Are different types of marital enrichment experiences more or less effective than others? Twelve of the forty studies (30%) have directly compared two types of marital enrichment programs. (See Table 1.)

Wieman (1973) contrasted the Conjugal Relationship Enhancement

(CRE) program, a behavioral exchange program, and a waiting list control group. Both enrichment programs resulted in significant increases in marital adjustment, in communication skill, and in target behaviors, and there were no differences between the two programs. Kilmann, Moreault, and Robinson (1978) and Kilmann, Julian, and Moreault (1978) contrasted two formats of the same program and a no-treatment control group. In both studies, the sequence of treatment experiences did not affect outcome, and both treatment formats were superior to no treatment. Two additional studies which used alternative treatments found, as did Wieman (1973), no differences among the various treatments (McIntosh, 1975; Williams, 1975). These studies, however, reported no significant changes for any of the enrichment experiences.

In contrast to these results, seven studies reported superiority of one treatment format over another. Epstein and Jackson (1978) included communication training, interaction-insight, and no-treatment groups in their study. Both treatment groups reduced verbal disagreements. Only the communication training group, however, led to increases in assertive requests, decreases in verbal attacks, and increases in spouse-rated empathy. Hines (1976) also reported superiority of a communication training experience over both an insight and a control group, using a rater's estimate of the couples' mutual helpfulness as the outcome measure. Three studies of the Minnesota Couples Communication Program (MCCP) have yielded data supporting the superiority of that particular communication enrichment program over alternative programs (Brown, 1976; Witkin, Note 6) or over another format of the MCCP (Beaver, 1978). Brown (1976) contrasted the MCCP, a marriage enrichment growth group, and a no treatment group and found significant changes in sex stereotyping of self and spouse only for couples in the MCCP group. Witkin (Note 6) reported significantly greater changes at post-test and two month follow-up on behavioral measures of nonverbal positives and both verbal and nonverbal negatives for his MCCP group than for a behaviorally oriented communication skill workshop group or a no treatment control group. Beaver (1978) compared two formats of the MCCP—one with couple participation and the other with each spouse in separate groups—and a no treatment group. Significant changes on self-report of communication and empathy occurred only for husbands in the conjoint participation condition.

Fischer (1973) found that a behaviorally oriented group made significant gains in prediction of attitudes and preferences of spouses relative to a conrtrol group and to a facilitative group based on Adlerian and functional methods. Finally, although Venema (1976) found very little change for any of these treatments, a combination of communication training and behavioral exchange led to greater change on a number of measures than did either communication training or behavioral exchange alone.

In summary, studies have been made comparing the effectiveness of different marital enrichment formats. The research suggests that communication training (Brown, 1976; Epstein and Jackson, 1978; Hines, 1976) and behavioral exchange (Fisher, 1973) are superior to insight-oriented group experiences. Specific contrasts of behavioral and communication-training programs have yielded mixed results (Venema, 1976; Wieman, 1973; Witkin, Note 6). We must, however, be cautious in making conclusions at this point, since the number of relevant studies is very small.

Do programs with different formats and content produce different types of changes? The comparative studies described provide no evidence for this possibility. Comparing the results of the various studies in Table 1 does, however, suggest a possible difference in the types of changes produced by different marital enrichment experiences. Positive changes on all three general types of outcome measures—marital adjustment, perceptual and personality measures, and relationship skill measures—have been obtained in many of the studies of communication training and behavior exchange programs. For programs consisting of mixed experiences and exercises, there is consistent evidence for positive change only on perceptual and personality measures. Of course, only two of the studies of the mixed type of enrichment experience have included both marital adjustment or relationship skill measures. So, we cannot draw any conclusions about different types of changes occurring with different programs until more comparative studies, which include all three types of outcome measures, have been completed.

For particular interventions that result in positive change, what are the effective components of the program that produce the change? For what types of participants are the enrichment programs effective? The studies by Beaver (1978) and Roberts (1975) are the only ones we have located which sought to identify an effective component of a marital enrichment experience. Roberts (1975) examined differences in outcome as a function of therapists' experience level, using novice paraprofessional, experienced paraprofessional, and graduate student therapists. He found that outcome was positively related to the experience level of the therapists, that is, the groups led by more experienced therapists had better outcome. Beaver (1978) found that changes in communication and empathy occurred when partners were in the same enrichment group but not when the partners participated in separate groups. Clearly, many other variables, for example, the inclusion or exclusion of specific exercises, the time format, number of leaders per group, and social class of participants (most programs have been limited to middle-class couples) need to be related to outcome.

Two studies have examined the response of different types of participants to marital enrichment experiences. Neville (1971) used the Myers Briggs Type Indicator to identify personality types among participants in a marital enrichment experience. He found that a significantly greater proportion of volunteer participants were intuitive-feeling types as opposed to sensing-thinking personality types. Neville concluded that these two personality types differed in their comfort and compatibility with the enrichment process, but that both groups, nevertheless, responded well to the experience.

Huber (Note 3) assessed the outcome of a Marriage Encounter experience using the Caring Relationship Inventory (CRI) (Shostrom, 1967). He reported that only the male participants showed significant positive change on CRI scales; females' scores did not change. Interestingly, Beaver (1978) found similar results. When partners participated in a communication group together, only the husbands showed significant changes on communication and empathy measures.

Thus, one of these studies (Neville, 1972) suggests that, although individuals with certain personality types may be more likely than others to volunteer for marital enrichment experiences, the outcome of the experience may not be affectd by the participant's personality type. The other two studies (Beaver, 1978; Huber, Note 3), on the other hand, suggest that males may be more likely than females to change following participation in at least some marital enrichment programs. More research is needed before we can determine whether enrichment programs are more or less effective for different types of participants.

We can conclude from this examination of the research that some optimism about the effectiveness of marital enrichment programs is warranted. We must, however, be very cautious in our optimism. Although generally positive results have been reported, we must await the presentation of more well-designed research before we can comfortably conclude that marital enrichment produces stable, positive change in couples.

Conclusion to Section I

If marriage enrichment or preventive marital health is to become a significant area of emphasis which impacts upon a truly broad spectrum of the population, some real changes will have to be made within and outside the movement. People within the movement will need to actively seek and open up their programs to the careful scrutiny of appropriate empirical research, so that we can identify the effective component parts of each program, and, as a result, create more effective and efficient programs. For this to happen, proponents of marriage enrichment will have to realize and accept the fact that the enthusiastic testimonies of participants and leaders is not sufficient (though the quantity of them requires careful notice). Explicit, carefully developed, and defined theoretical frameworks for the various programs and techniques used need to be developed. Some of the almost fanatical, cult-like, "ours is the best program," enthusiasm will have to be replaced with a more open and flexible attitude which is based upon matching programs to the specific needs and abilities of specific individuals and couples. The need for appropriate and ongoing training of nonprofessional and professional leaders must continue to be addressed, with an emphasis on the cognitive and theoretical areas as well as the experiential and interpersonal relations areas.

The professional community of marital and family counselors, therapists, researchers, and educators will need to truly accept and acknowledge that significant learning, change, and growth can occur within a learning experience led by (and even created by) nonprofessionals. With that acceptance can come open support of such programs and a specific and planned effort to utilize professional skills in the development and training of appropriate nonprofessional leaders (L'Abate, 1977a).

We wonder why the helping professions have been so slow to accept the viability of a marital health or marriage enrichment approach to dyadic interactions and relationships. Part of the answer may lie in the failure of many proponents of marriage enrichment to have been seriously concerned with approprite research and theoretical considerations. However, that is possibly only part of the reason. Clark Vincent (1973, 1977) has raised some questions along these same lines. Could there also be fears of diminished stature on the part of professionals? (i.e., "If they can really help themselves so much, or can be helped by someone with much less training than I have, then what will happen to me?") Could there be fears that if people can be helped by marital enrichers, all that will be left for the trained professional therapist will be the very difficult cases (Vincent, 1973)?

We believe there will always be a need for the highly skilled, trained, and qualified professionals in the field of marital and relationship therapy. Many people simply cannot benefit from marriage enrichment experiences, or cannot benefit from them as much as from conjoint or individual therapy. But, can the trained professional be contented with the offering of these traditional services? We think not, especially if research demonstrates that a marriage enrichment or preventive marital health approach is as helpful and efficient, or more so than, traditional methods, and can provide a helpful adjunct to therapy. If this is the case, then there is a need for the trained professional therapist to learn and develop specific skills in preventive marital health and marriage enrichment in order to help couples to develop their potential for effective relationships (Wright and L'Abate, 1977).

With the acceptance of a philosophy of prevention and marriage enrichment by the professional community, it is hoped that marital health could be developed as a multidisciplinary and inter-professional specialty field (Vincent, 1973, 1977), and that appropriate degree programs in the area of enrichment could be developed (L'Abate, 1977a). But even without the establishment of a separate specialty field or degree programs, there is a current need for the various training programs in marriage counseling to focus on marital enrichment and preventive marital health. Trainees need to be exposed to growth-oriented and preventive approaches and models as well as to models which focus upon the treatment of dysfunctional relationships or systems. That exposure needs to include appropriate theory and practical experiences, with couples in therapy as well as those from the broader community (cf. Guldner, 1978).

Agencies which serve the family need to be encouraged to include positive and preventive programming in their services to clinical and nonclinical populations. Marriage enrichment programming needs to be extended to those preparing for marriage and to senior citzens (Mace and Mace, 1977). The lack of a specific focus on sexuality in many marriage enrichment programs needs to be corrected (Otto, 1975).

The list could go on indefinitely, but, in brief, what is needed is for the various proponents and practitioners of marriage enrichment (professional and nonprofessional) and marital counselors, therapists, researchers, and educators to join in a truly collaborative and concerted effort to make the potential benefits of marriage enrichment available to all couples who could benefit from such a service. A united effort, welcomed and sought by both groups, could conceivably exert significant political pressure, could encourage the federal government to develop a focused emphasis and policy on marriage (Mace and Mace, 1975), and could tap the financial and personnel resources of various government agencies to provide positive, growth-oriented services.

As some of these hopes and dreams become realities, preventive marital health and marriage enrichment will achieve a new and deeper level of significance in our society. The development, implementation, and assimilation of a growth-oriented marital philosophy throughout our society could have a significant impact upon marital and family life in the future. But, in the final analysis, it will take commitment on the part of individual couples to the ongoing process of marriage enrichment. For most couples that will mean a disciplined involvement in a personally meaningful program designed to enable the participants to fulfill their potential as individuals and as a married couple.

The Creative Marriage Enrichment Program

This section of the book deals with the marriage enrichment program used at the Marriage Council of Philadelphia. We present here the foundation of our program, as well as a detailed description of the actual exercises and experiences used, including samples of program handouts.

Introduction to Section II

Section II describes the Creative Marriage Enrichment Program that I designed with my wife, Millie Hof. The program is currently being used for clinical and nonclinical couples at the Marriage Council of Philadelphia. Facilitators have been trained in the use of this particular marriage enrichment model, as well as in the philosophy and process of marriage enrichment described in Section I. They are currently conducting programs in marriage enrichment in various community and church settings.

The Creative Mariage Enrichment Program has been designed to help the participants to experience their marital relationship as something which is continually growing and being recreated. The program is based on the belief that marital relationships are dynamic, not static, and that change in such relationships is not only possible, but inevitable. It is also believed that change can be a positive and growing force if individuals and couples are willing to assume the responsibility of becoming effective agents of change, if they develop the skills needed to make that possible, and if they continue to use those skills in a committed, disciplined, and patient way. When these actions take place in an atmosphere of mutual empathy, trust, understanding, and peer support, couples have a maximum opportunity to deepen and enrich their lives together.

The Creative Marriage Enrichment Program attempts to provide such an atmosphere and to provide couples with an opportunity to develop their already existing relationship-enhancing skills and to learn new skills in areas such as communication, conflict resolution, and intimacy. There is an emphasis on 1) expressing feelings, wants, and needs; 2) identifying, expressing, and affirming individual and marital strengths; 3) understanding and negotiating gender roles in marriage; 4) creatively using conflict; and 5) exploring various facts of intimacy.

The purpose of enriching a couple's life together through a process of self-reflection and reflection upon their marital relationship is accomplished through a variety of experiential exercises. Some aspects of the exercises focus upon the individual and are designed to help each person to experience himself or herself as a unique individual within a relationship. This increases individuation and reduces "couplism," or the tendency to always identify with the *we* aspects of the marital relationship. On the other hand, the exercises that focus on the couple are designed to help the participants to experience each other as two persons in specific relationship to each other, with a unique life as a couple. The multi-couple or total group exercises are designed for couples to experience the possibility and reality of support, feedback and caring from other persons and couples. As that is accomplished, our societally scripted sense of privatism (which states that anything about the marriage stays within the marriage) is reduced.

The program was born in 1972 in St. Andrew's United Methodist Church in Warminster, Pennsylvania. It emerged out of the expressed need of several couples to experience more life and joy in their marriages. Since its beginning, the program has undergone many changes and revisions, reaching its present form in 1977. Like an effective marital relationship, however, the program is constantly growing and changing, and it will probably never reach a truly final form.

Our hope in presenting the program through this book is that it will ultimately help some people to discover the fulfillment of being involved in a dynamic marital relationship that is renewed over and over again. We have experienced that process to be joyful at times, and painful on other occasions. There have been moments of extreme closeness, love, and deep satisfaction, as well as times of conflicted distance and frustration. But through it all, there has also been a commitment to growth: growth as individuals, growth as a couple, and growth as a family. It is that commitment to growth and renewal which we believe characterizes an effective marriage, and which the Creative Marriage Enrichment Program endeavors to actualize.

Section II of this book first examines the theoretical foundation of the Creative Marriage Enrichment Program and describes the emphasis on the couple's inclusion, control, and affection needs. We also discuss the rationale for the program's use of varied, structured experiences and the flexibility of the program for use in a variety of settings. Then we present the specific exercises of the Creative Marriage Enrichment Program which focuses on inclusion, control, and affection needs. These final chapters are written in a program manual format so that the reader can actually use selected exercises or the entire program.

Before proceeding with our examination of the Creative Marriage Enrichment Program, one disclaimer is in order. Although we emphasized in a previous chapter of this book the importance of evaluating the effects of marriage enrichment programs through careful research, our belief and confidence in our program is based not on research, but on personal experiences with the program and with the many couples who have participated in it. At the time of this writing, we are conducting three major empirical studies which assess the impact of the program on both clinical and nonclinical couples. Although we are confident of the value of the Creative Marriage Enrichment Program, and we expect our research to confirm our experiences, we recognize that, as with most of the other programs currently in use, a definitive statement on the effectiveness of the program must await the completion of objective, scientific research.

۶ 6

The Creative Marriage Enrichment Program: Theoretical Foundation

The Creative Marriage Enrichment Program shares three theoretical roots that are common to virtually all marriage enrichment programs (see Chapter 1). First, there is the *Rogerian emphasis* on providing an empathic environment in which participants can freely express their feelings and experience increased self-acceptance, self-knowledge, and acceptance of and from others, especially their spouse. The assumption is made that experiences of this nature within an empathic environment will contribute to changes in cognition and the attitudes which underlie behavior (Guerney, 1977) and will thereby lead the participants to change their behavior.

Secondly, there is the *behavioral emphasis* on enabling participants to learn and practice specific skills they can use to change their own behavior. Here, it is assumed that repeated practice and reinforcement will help correct deficiencies in social learning and will lead to enduring positive change. There is an emphasis on increasing behaviors perceived to be desirable, helpful, and rewarding in the marriage relationship (e.g., positive statements, ownership and expression of feelings, effective contracting and negotiation skills).

Thirdly, there is an emphasis on the use of *group process* to provide an environment in which various curative (Yalom, 1970) and growth factors (Egan, 1970) can be experienced (e.g., sense of universality, imitative behavior, interpersonal learning, supportive atmosphere). The group setting provides a temporary and safe learning environment, through which trust can grow and from which support can be drawn. In addition, couples have the opportunity to observe alternative models of relating and to give and receive appropriate feedback.

In addition to these three roots or foundation stones, the Creative Marriage Enrichment Program is based upon Schutz's (1966, 1973, 1978) assumption that all individuals have three basic interpersonal needs which are manifested in various behaviors and feelings in the individuals' relationships with other people. Schutz believes these three basic needs—inclusion, control and affection—"are rooted in a person's feelings about himself, his self-concept" (Schutz, 1973, p. 414). He has expressed the intrapersonal dimensions of these needs in the following manner:

Inclusion refers to feelings about being important or significant, or worthwhile. *Control* refers to feelings of competence, including intelligence, appearance, practicality and general ability to cope with the world. *Affection* revolves around feelings of being lovable, of feeling that if one's personal essence is revealed in its entirety it will be seen as a lovely thing (Schutz, 1973, p. 414).

Schutz assumes that all human interaction may be categorized according to these three needs, and he has behaviorally defined the interpersonal dimensions of each of them.

The interpersonal need for *inclusion* is the need to establish and maintain a satisfactory relationship with people with respect to interaction and association. Some terms that connote various aspects of a relationship that is primarily positive inclusion are 'associate, interact, mingle, communicate, belong, companion, comrade, attend to, member, togetherness, join, extrovert, pay attention to, interested, encounter'. Negative inclusion is connoted by 'exclude, isolate, outsider, outcast, lonely, detached, withdrawn, abandon, ignore' (Schutz, 1978, p. 8).

The need for inclusion varies on a continuum from undersocial to oversocial, and the core problem of inclusion can be expressed as *in* or *out*. One of the key aspects of inclusion is that of having a unique identity (Schutz, 1973). "An integral part of being recognized and paid attention to is that the individual be uniquely distinguishable from other people. The height of being identifiable is to be understood, since it implies that someone is interested enough to discover a person's unique characteristics" (Schutz, 1973, p. 414).

The interpersonal need for *control* is defined as:

the need to establish and maintain a satisfactory relationship with people with respect to control and power. Control behavior refers to the decision-making process between people. Some terms that connote aspects of primarily positive control are: 'power, authority, dominance, influence, control, ruler, superior, officer, leader'. Aspects of negative control are connoted by 'rebellion, resistance, follower, anarchy, submissive, henpecked, milquetoast' (Schutz, 1978, p. 8).

The need for control varies on a continuum from the desire to control other people and have authority over them (autocrat) to the desire to be controlled and have someone else be responsible for one's life (abdicrat). The core problem of control can be expressed as *top* or *bottom* (Schutz, 1973).

The interpersonal need for *affection* is defined as:

the need to establish and maintain a satisfactory relationship with others with respect to love and affection. Some terms that connote aspects of primarily positive affection are 'love, like, emotionally close, personal, intimate, friend, sweetheart'. Aspects of negative affection are connoted by 'hate, cool, dislike, emotionally distant, rejection' (Schutz, 1978, p. 8).

The need for affection varies on a continuum from the underpersonal, with an avoidance of feeling involvement, to the overpersonal. The core problem of affection can be expressed as *close* or *far* (Schutz, 1973).

Inclusion needs must be addressed especially when a relationship is being formed, but inclusion needs must also continue to be addressed as a relationship continues to grow and develop. Control and affection needs are generally manifested in relationships that have already been formed (Schutz, 1973). We believe that effective resolution of inclusion needs precedes resolution of control needs. Control needs, in turn, must be resolved in order for the persons in a relationship to develop their potential for intimacy (affection) to its fullest extent. In the Creative Marriage Enrichment Program, therefore, we focus on the area of inclusion first, control second, and affection third. It must be emphasized, however, that these three needs are interdependent and overlap and intersect with each other, and all three are continually being addressed, even simultaneously, in any given relationship. The concept then is one of an overlapping, forward moving, spiral, rather than a model of strict linearity, with A preceding B preceding C.

Although these theoretical concepts which form one part of the theoretical base of the Creative Marriage Enrichment Program are drawn almost exclusively from the work of Schutz, it should be stressed that they have also been identified by other researchers and clinicians to be central dimensions of interpersonal relating. For example, Horowitz (1979) conducted an empirical study designed to identify the core interpersonal relationship problems or themes of individuals beginning psychotherapy. Three central themes emerged from this study: the degree of psychological involvement between the subject and the other person; the nature of the involvement from friendly to hostile; and the subject's intention to influence, change or control the other person. As Horowitz noted, these dimensions are quite similar to those postulated by Schutz (1966, 1973, 1978). In addition, Berman and Lief (1975), in their discussion of marital psychodynamics, noted that marital and other dyadic relationships involve the dimensions of power, intimacy, and inclusion-exclusion. Their definitions of these dimensions are also extremely similar to those of Schutz.

In order for a relationship to be mutually satisfying and fulfilling, the persons involved in it must come to grips with these issues of inclusion, control, and affection and resolve them in ways they find appropriate and meaningful. In individuals and relationships that are in a constant state of development (Berman and Lief, 1975; Levinson, 1978; Sheehy, 1974; Widick and Cowan, 1977) these needs have differing levels of intensity and urgency at different points in time. At one point in the individual or relationship life cycle, inclusion needs may be in the foreground. At another point, intimacy or affection needs may require the most attention. Therefore, any resolution of these issues needs to be viewed as immediate, dynamic, and subject to change, as the individual and relationship needs change and develop over time, rather than as rigid, inflexible, and set in stone.

As Berman and Lief (1975) note, the dynamic forces in marriage "result from each spouse's need to achieve his or her expectations . . . offset and opposed by the need to compromise or submerge these desires in order to enable the partner to attain his or her expectations" (p. 585) in these central dimensions of interpersonal need and interpersonal relating.

Each individual must, therefore, develop an appropriate and satisfying balance in his life with regard to these needs of inclusion, control, and affection. To do that effectively within the context of a marital relationship requires self-awareness and self-esteem as well as awareness of, and respect and esteem for, the other person in the relationship. Differences between one's own needs and desires as well as differences between partners, lead to inevitable internal and interpersonal conflicts. These differences need to be addressed openly and directly in order for satisfying dynamic solutions to be achieved. In order for that to occur, individuals and couples must be encouraged and enabled to explore *all three* of these areas of interpersonal need. They also need to be encouraged and taught skills that will facilitate the development of an appropriate and satisfying balance, and, through that balance, a fulfilling marital relationship. The achievement of that goal is the ultimate aim of the Creative Marriage Enrichment Program.

THE USE OF STRUCTURED EXPERIENCES

Marriage enrichment programs vary in their degree of structure. The degree of structure varies on a continuum ranging from highly structured and couple-centered, some almost to the point of being programmed instruction, to relatively nonstructured and centered on the couple-group. The Creative Marriage Enrichment Program can be placed on the middle third of the continuum. When used strictly as described in the following chapters, in a weekend setting, employing the minimum time allocations, the program would be placed towards the structured and couple-centered end of the continuum. When used over a fifteen week period, using larger time allocations or open-ended time blocks, and adding units of unstructured couple-group time, the program would be located more towards the nonstructured end of the continuum.

Structured experiences, those that use specific directions for the participants to follow, are employed for a variety of reasons. The research and theoretical formulations of Bednar, Melnick, and Kaul (1974) and Goldstein, Heller, and Sechrest (1966) suggest that leaders should use a high degree of structure early in group counseling and psychotherapy and then use a diminishing amount of structure as the group develops over time.

Kurtz (1975) has reviewed the research on the use of structured experiences in groups and has pointed out the consistency in the results. Structured experiences have been reported to lead to greater group cohesiveness, greater involvement of the participants in group activities, participants viewing leaders in a more favorable light, and participant self-reports of greater learning from the group experiences (Kurtz, 1975). In addition, the evidence indicates that factors other than the use of specific techniques (e.g., the facilitator) lead to changes in participants. Since creating an environment in which cohesiveness, member involvement, and interpersonal trust are especially important in the early stages of a group's development and since the use of structured experiences contributes to the development of this kind of atmosphere and environment, structured experiences can most effectively be used early in a group's development.

Since the Creative Marriage Enrichment Program is a relatively brief, time-limited, basic experience, usually attended by people who have virtually no history together as a group, the use of structured experiences provides an effective means for addressing group development needs, while at the same time focusing upon various issues of importance to marital growth and development. However, when we work with a group that continues its life beyond the basic experience, we employ fewer and fewer structured experiences, moving more towards a non-structured, interactionally oriented model with an emphasis on open sharing and couple dialogue within a group setting (Mace and Mace, 1976b).

THE USE OF A VARIETY OF EXPERIENCES

The exercises which comprise the Creative Marriage Enrichment Program vary in terms of both their specific aims and their experiential format and structure. A major reason for varying the experiential format of the exercises is to take advantage of the fact that different individuals vary in their preferred learning styles. As a consequence of hereditary factors and socialization experiences, individuals develop learning styles that are more influenced by certain learning abilities than by others (Kolb, 1979).

A number of cognitive theorists have suggested primary dimensions that underlie the learning process and have categorized the learning process according to different types of learning abilities (e.g., Kagan and Kogan,

1970; Kolb, 1979; Piaget, 1970). Kolb (1979) has identified four kinds of learning abilities: 1) concrete experience in which the person is fully and openly involved in new experiences; 2) reflective observation where the individual observes and reflects on experiences from new and different perspectives; 3) abstract conceptualization in which the person creates concepts that integrate his observations; and 4) active experimentation where theories are used to make decisions or attempt solutions to problems.

Participants in a marriage enrichment program typically are a heterogeneous group of people, differing with regard to their strengths in each of the types of learning abilities. Therefore, for maximum learning to occur, it is important that the program include experiences and exercises that are varied in the type of learning ability emphasized. When a program is structured in this way, we can be more certain that every participant's learning style will be compatible with at least some of the exercises.

Specific examples of how certain experiences in the Creative Marriage Enrichment Program differ in their emphasis on the various types of learning abilities may be useful. The Pleasuring exercise (see page 138) involves the couple sitting facing each other silently, getting in touch with feelings of warmth for the other person, and then giving a gentle facial massage. The objectives of this exercise are to experience and receive feelings of intimacy in a nonverbal, physical way, and to increase bonding in the relationship through the sharing of unconditional positive regard. This requires the utilization of the concrete experience learning ability in that each person becomes fully involved in a new experience. The use of the reflective observation learning skill is exemplified in the Marriage Life Line. (See page 91.) In this experience, each partner draws a marriage life-line, including high and low points, happy, sad, hurt, turbulent times, and so forth, and then shares and discusses the drawings. Thus, the couple is observing and reflecting on their experiences from new and different perspectives in order to increase their sense of inclusion, to share their feelings about marital experiences, and to increase their ability to listen accurately and empathetically to each other.

At different points throughout the Creative Marriage Enrichment Program, brief discussions of new concepts or theoretical formulations are presented to the couple. For example, the "Inclusion, Control, Affection" discussion briefly presents Schutz's (1966, 1971, 1973, 1978) theory that inclusion, control, and affection are primary dimensions of any relationship. The discussions capitalize on the individuals' abstract conceptualization learning ability in that the individuals are provided with concepts by which they can integrate their observations.

The fourth learning skill, active experimentation, is represented in the Contract Writing exercise. (See page 104.) In this exercise, couples share wants, needs, and fears in some specified area and then agree on and write a specific, achievable, time-oriented contract for changing one thing that they would like to be different. Clearly, this exercise requires the couple to actively experiment with the theory of contract writing in order to make decisions and attempt solutions to problems.

In summary, different individuals are seen as having characteristic learning styles that result from differing strengths and weaknesses in the four basic learning skills. In order to maximize the potential for learning for all individuals and couples, the Creative Marriage Enrichment Program includes a variety of exercises. Some of the exercises emphasize one or another particular learning ability, whereas other exercises require utilization of some combination of the learning abilities in order for the exercise objectives to be achieved.

VARIETY OF SETTINGS

The Creative Marriage Enrichment Program can be used in a variety of ways and settings. We have no presumptuous belief that this program is the *best* or most effective marriage enrichment program available. What we do believe, however, is that it is *a* model (one of many) that many people have found helpful in facilitating and contributing to the growth and development of their marital relationship. Since it is *a* model, and not *the* model, we encourage experienced facilitators who use it to experiment with the program design by making thoughtful and carefully planned additions or deletions, alterations or modifications to the program to suit the special needs of a particular group of couples. For example, individuals and couples differ in their psychosocial and cognitive levels of development (Widick and Cowan, 1977), as well as in their levels of individual and relationship function/dysfunction. (See Chapter 3.) Facilitators will need to modify the program as they work with couples at these different levels. In addition, program changes may also be needed to bring the model in line with the facilitator's own theoretical orientation.

We have found that the program fits comfortably into a weekend retreat or conference setting, beginning Friday evening and ending before the evening meal on Sunday. We prefer to work with a group composed of eight to ten participant couples and one leadership couple. However, we have effectively used the program with groups as small as six couples and as large as fifty-five couples. When the program is used in this way, couples have the opportunity to be together as a couple, away from normal routines, constraints, and pressures, in an atmosphere of seclusion and leisure, to take a continuous and intensive look at the marriage relationship, and to work with other couples on enhancing the relationship. The intensive nature of the experience, as well as the positive, affective and behavioral emphasis and growth orientation, frequently leads to a highly satisfying emotional experience for participants, especially as they realize that positive change is possible. Many couples report a renewed and deepened sense of intimacy and commitment to the relationship, as well as an expanded view of the potential and strength of the relationship. Such a weekend experience, however, provides only a limited amount of time for couples to be introduced to, and practice, a variety of relationship-enhancing skills.

Although there is often an increase in motivation for, and commitment to, positive change and the development of needed skills, integration of these skills and the changing of long-standing patterns of marital interaction do not occur through one weekend-long experience. Such an initial marital enrichment or marital growth experience must be followed by a continuing and disciplined use of those skills. Therefore, it needs to be emphasized that, when this program is used in a weekend-setting, the experience is only one part of the ongoing process of marriage enrichment.

The major result of such a weekend experience may be the positive attitudinal change and the increased motivation for growth and development of the relationship reported by many couples. Granted, this is not the same as stable, enduring, integrated, behavioral change. However, anyone who has attempted to teach a couple new behavioral skills when motivation and hope for change are low and attitudes are somewhat less than positive knows how difficult, if not impossible, the process can be. Thus, when used as a weekend experience, the Creative Marriage Enrichment Program can be viewed as a *motivational program,* and as an *introduction* to relationship enhancing skills. It should then be followed by intensive, specific skill training, and an ongoing or time-limited support group or marital growth group of sufficient duration and depth to permit needed practice and integration of skills to occur. If there is no such skill training, follow-up, or support group provided after the initial experience, the shock of return to the realities of everyday life can be somewhat painful, leaving the couple with a feeling of isolation and frustration. As noted earlier, in such a situation, positive gains from the weekend experience can quickly fade, feelings of failure can emerge, and integration of learning and skills frequently does not occur.

For these reasons, some facilitators prefer to use this program over a number of weeks (8–15), employing two-hour to four-hour sessions. The suggested advantages of the multiweek approach are spaced learning, continuing reinforcement and support from peers, the opportunity to do homework between meetings and practice new skills, the ability to devote a greater amount of time to the development, practice, and integration of specific skills, the ability to utilize more unstructured group and couple interaction time, and the possibility of maintaining the momentum and continuing the group as an unstructured, ongoing, peer-led, marital support or growth group after the initial time-limited program has been completed. Disadvantages might include a lack of intensity, broken continuity, and the possible contamination of the process by the normal routines, commitments, pressures, and responsibilities of daily life. Here again, even with a multi-week approach, the emphasis needs to be made that the initial program is only one part of the ongoing process of marriage enrichment. Continual commitment to marital growth, disciplined use of appropriate skills, and participation in periodic experiential education experiences, possibly even a monthly, peer-led marital support group, contribute to maintaining positive attitudes toward each other and the marriage and to maintaining the behavioral skills needed to produce enduring change and marital satisfaction.

More and more proponents of marriage enrichment are suggesting a combination of both models (Hopkins et al, 1978). At the Marriage Council of Philadelphia, we are currently conducting research to identify the differential effects, if any, of various combinations and sequences of marriage enrichment experiences upon particular individuals and couples. We hypothesize that the experience of stable, enduring, positive behavioral and attitudinal change through marriage enrichment programming can be most effectively achieved in three basic steps. Participation in an intensive, broad-based, issue-oriented program should be a first step. This initial experience can generate a high level of positive feeling between partners and a positive attitude towards the relationship. It can increase motivation, and contribute to change and can begin the development of relationship-enhancing skills. The first step soon should be followed by a sharply focused, time-limited, multi-week, communication-training program. The belief is that the positive feelings and heightened motivations will contribute to the commitment and discipline needed for effective, intensive communication training, which in turn is crucial for the development of any further relationship-enhancing skills (e.g., conflict utilization). Finally, couples can then receive and give continuing support and reinforcement and experience further skill development through participation in an ongoing, monthly, peer-led marital growth or support group, and other periodic marital growth experiences (e.g., sexual enrichment program).

The Creative Marriage Enrichment Program: Inclusion

The interpersonal need for *inclusion* is the need to establish and maintain a satisfactory relationship with people with respect to interaction and 'association. Some terms that connote various aspects of positive inclusion are associate, interact, mingle, communicate, belong, companion, comrade, attend to, member, togetherness, join, extrovert, pay attention to, interested, and encounter' (Schutz, 1978, p. 8).

The first section of the Creative Marriage Enrichment Program is designed primarily to address this interpersonal need for inclusion. The following sequence of exercises is presented as if the decision has been made to conduct the program over a weekend, from Friday evening to Sunday evening. See Appendix A for an overview of such a design.

ARRIVAL, CHECK-IN, AND COFFEE TIME

Couples are instructed to arrive approximately forty-five minutes before the scheduled starting time of the program. This gives them the opportunity to register, to unpack (if the program involves staying overnight), to relax with a cup of coffee, and to begin to turn their thinking away from concerns such as work, family, or home, and focus towards the marital relationship.

We believe that openness, appropriate sharing and modeling by the leadership couple or team throughout the program are facilitative and highly valued by the participant couples. This modeling begins with the initial contact with the participants, and is conveyed through appropriate attention to details, clear instructions, friendly greetings, and other relatively minor things even before the actual program begins. Of course, it continues throughout the program as the leadership couple demonstrates in an open, and appropriately risking and vulnerable way the kind of interaction and caring that is requested of the participants.

INTRODUCTION

Time: Ten minutes.

Procedure: During the introductory period, the leadership couple or team introduce themselves and briefly introduce the program. Details regarding the location of restrooms, meal times, break times, availability of refreshments, and so on, are also attended to at this time. The general purpose of the Creative Marriage Enrichment Program is posted on newsprint and shared with the group: "to deepen and enrich our life together as a couple through a process of self-reflection and reflection upon our marital relationship." Personal comfort is stressed, as is the voluntary nature of all experiences. Participants are encouraged to participate in all experiences, but are also given clear permission not to participate in any given experience without the need for any explanation to the leadership couple or team. The fact that all total group interaction is purely voluntary and that couples do most of the exercises by themselves somewhat diminishes the role peer pressure can play in forcing individuals or couples to disclose themselves beyond the point where they are comfortable.

GOAL-SETTING

Objectives: The objectives for the Goal-Setting experience are to identify individual wants and couple wants from this marriage enrichment program, to develop a sense of individuation and differentiation within the marital relationship, and to interact with another couple to expand the boundaries of sharing regarding the marital relationship (beginning to build a sense of a group and reducing our societally scripted sense of privatism).

·Time: Thirty-five minutes.

Procedure: For ten minutes, each individual is requested to list two things in a spiral notebook: "What I want for myself from this marriage enrichment experience is . . . ;" and "What I want for my marriage from this marriage enrichment experience is . . ." Each person is to compile as extensive a list as they desire. For the next ten minutes, each couple briefly shares and discusses the individual lists. Then they are instructed to make a list in which is stated at least one want for each individual and at least two wants for their marriage that they as a couple agree upon. For the last fifteen minutes, two couples meet, introduce themselves, share something about themselves that the others don't already know, and then share their individual and cou-

---

*A note regarding instructions is in order here. We have found that the giving of instructions can consume a disproportionate amount of time. Therefore, it is crucial that the facilitators be quite familiar with the design of each experience within the program. We have also found it extremely helpful to have as many of the instructions as possible printed and posted on newsprint. This enables the participants to have continued reference to them during each experience.

ple wants or goals with each other. Each person is requested to share at least their own individual goal with the other people. This prevents one member of the couple from doing all of the talking for the couple. The experience ends with the four people identifying and verbalizing one feeling they have as they finish this first task.

COMMUNICATION SKILLS

Objectives: The objectives for the Communication Skills experience are to increase the ability to listen attentively, accurately and affectively, to increase the ability to accurately and verbally reflect back what was heard, and to share some personal goals, dreams and feelings to deepen the communication level between partners.

Time: Fifty minutes.

Procedure: A brief (ten minutes) discussion is given regarding effective communication, which is defined as "common meaning" (i.e., what is intended is sent, and what is received is the original, intended message). Various dimensions and levels of communication are described and illustrated, such as content and process (what is said versus how it is said), verbal and nonverbal aspects (words, tone, and inflection versus body language), the interpersonal, intrapersonal, and environmental dimensions (e.g., effect of a smoke-filled room upon communication), and the cognitive and affective levels (effective use of thoughts and feelings). Effective communication is described as including awareness of, and appropriate utilization of, all of these dimensions and levels of communication. Two core communication skills are defined as listening (hearing what the other person is saying to us) and speaking (sending a straight, clear message). The importance of effective communication in building and maintaing satisfactory marital relationships is also stressed.

The discussion is followed by a forty minute skill practice session, focusing on parroting, paraphrasing and total listening. The sequence used involves definition of parroting, paraphrasing or total listening, brief practice, and total group response to questions such as, "What did you experience?," "What was easy or difficult?", and "What made it easy or difficult?"

PARROTING

The group is requested to define the word parroting. One of the leaders then defines it as, "saying back exactly what the speaker said, word for word." The leadership couple demonstrates parroting (e.g., Partner #1, "My individual goal for this marriage enrichment experience is to learn how to communicate more effectively with you, especially with feelings." Partner #2, "Your individual goal for this marriage enrichment experience is to learn how to communicate more effectively with me, especially with feelings."). After the leadership couple has demonstrated parroting, the participant couples practice. One person in each couple begins the skill practice segment by saying and completing the statement, "My individual goal for this marriage enrichment experience is . . ." The listener parrots what he or she has heard. (Some listeners find it more meaningful to change the pronouns when parroting back what was heard. In such an instance, all other words would be parroted verbatim. For example, *"Your* individual goal for this . . .") The speaker indicates whether or not the listener has parroted what was originally said. If not, the process is repeated until the listener has accurately parroted the speaker's original message. When that task has been successfully accomplished, roles are reversed, and the same procedure is followed until a successful outcome has been achieved. The total group then briefly reflects upon what was easy, difficult, and so on.

PARAPHRASING

The group is requested to define the word paraphrasing. One of the leaders then defines it as, "saying back in your own words what you heard the speaker say." The leadership couple demonstrates paraphrasing (e.g., Partner #1, "One dream I've had about our marriage is that we could just leave the kids with your parents for two weeks, fly to Bermuda, and just sit on the beach and dance and just be together without any interruptions." Partner #2, "One dream you've had about our marriage is that we could take off to Bermuda, without the kids, and just be together, enjoying each other's company and doing what we want to do, without any interruptions."). After the leadership couple has demonstrated paraphrasing, the participant couples practice. One person in each couple begins the skill practice segment by saying and completing the statement, "One dream I've had about our marriage is . . . ." The listener paraphrases what he or she has heard. The speaker indicates whether or not the listener has paraphrased accurately what was originally said. If not, the process is repeated until the listener has accurately paraphrased the speaker's original message. When that task has been successfully accomplished, roles are reversed, and the same procedure is followed until a successful outcome has been achieved. The total group then briefly reflects upon what was easy or difficult and what made it so.

TOTAL LISTENING

The group is requested to define the phrase total listening (Egan, 1970). One of the leaders then defines it as, "being aware of the total person, what is being said verbally and nonverbally, and what is not being said, such as unexpressed feelings, hidden messages, etc. It involves my listening to you with my ears, my eyes, and sometimes my touch. It involves my listening to you and listening to your impact upon me in my thoughts, my feelings and my body as I listen to you. Total listening involves all of me with all of you—hearing you and myself." The leadership couple demonstrates total listening (e.g., Partner #1, looking sad, "A feeling I've had about myself recently is one of inadequacy—that I'm not as good of a husband as I'd like to be and as you want." Partner #2, reaching out and touching partner #1's hands, "Recently you've been feeling inadequate as a husband, and you sense that I want more from you and that you want to give more. I sense that realization makes you sad, and I feel your sadness."). After the leadership couple has demonstrated total listening, the participant couples practice. One person in each couple begins the skill practice segment by saying and completing the statement, "A feeling I've had about myself recently is . . ." The listener reflects back what was heard using the principle of total listening. The speaker indicates whether or not the listener has totally listened and reflected back what was originally said. If not, the process is repeated until the listener has accurately reflected the speaker's original message. When that task has been successfully completed, roles are reversed, and the same procedure is followed until a successful outcome has been achieved. The total group then briefly reflects upon what was easy or difficult, and what made it so. In this final total group segment, participants are also asked to compare their experiences with all three of the skill practice segments.

The total group reflection time gives individuals and couples the opportunity to generate and verbalize insights and to learn from each other. Comments emerge such as: "I realize how important it is to send short messages if I want to be heard," and "I have difficulty sensing the feelings because I am so wrapped up in just hearing and remembering the words." Participants are encouraged to practice the three skills throughout the weekend, and prior to each subsequent experience they are reminded to do so.

GROUP CIRCLE

Objective: The objective of the Group Circle experience is to contribute to the formation of a group sense of "we-ness" and unity, which includes the potential for touch.

Time: Ten minutes.

Procedure: The participants are requested to form a circle with arms around each other's waists, and to look around the circle, making eye contact with as many people as possible. The group then drops arms, and turns to the right. Each person then gently massages the shoulders and neck of the person in front of him or her. After a few minutes, each person does an about-face and repeats the process. After a few minutes (and usually many moans and groans of satisfaction), the circle is formed again with arms around each other's waists. Eye contact is once again made, arms are dropped, and the group is dismissed. (With religiously oriented groups, voluntary, individual, verbal sentence prayers—with open or closed eyes— frequently add a dimension of spiritual intimacy to the group's life, contributing to the development of a common bond in the group.) If the program is being conducted over a weekend, this experience completes Friday evening.

WAKE-UP EXERCISES

Objectives: The objectives of the Wake-Up Exercises are to wake-up the body and increase alertness by stimulating body muscles and increasing the blood flow to all parts of the body, and to involve the body (and not just the mind) in the enrichment process, emphasizing and modeling the unity of the person.

Time: Fifteen minutes.

Procedure: A variety of body awareness activities can be used in this time period, including the following:

1) light slapping of the entire body, from the top of the head to the soles of the feet, producing a tingling effect throughout the body

2) stretching of the arms, fingers, legs, torso, etc., including the vocal chords in waking-up sounds (e.g., yawns, groans, etc.)

3) flopping of the body, which involves bending forward at the waist, legs slightly apart, knees slightly bent, and flopping the upper torso rag-doll fashion, with arms and head hanging loosely, after which the person rises very slowly to an erect position

MARRIAGE LIFE LINE

Objectives: The objectives of the Marriage Life Line experience are to identify and share perceptions of the marriage, grounding the relationship in a historical past, present, and future, to identify and share feelings associated with marital experiences, and to increase the ability to listen accurately and empathetically to each other.

Time: Thirty-five minutes.

Procedure: Each participant is given a legal-size or longer piece of paper, and a large assortment of crayons is placed in the midst of the group for participants to use. Each individual is instructed to take fifteen minutes to think about and draw a marriage life line which represents his view of the marriage. Using words, phrases, stick figures, symbolic colors, and so on, the participants express in a visual form, significant events, happy, sad, hurtful, or turbulent times, and show their perception of past, present and future directions of the marriage relationship.

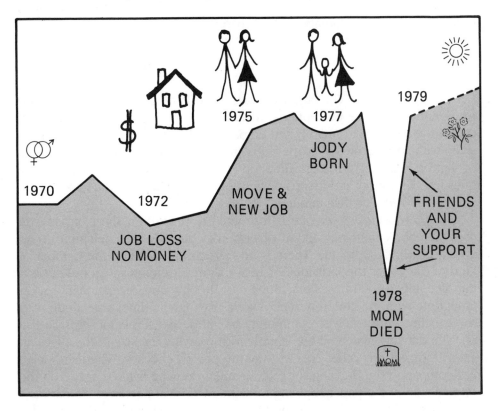

Figure 7.1. *Marriage Life Line*

After each person has made a drawing, each couple shares together what they intended to express in the drawing. Each partner shares, and the other's sole responsibility is to listen to what the speaker is saying. Questions are permitted to increase understanding, but participants are urged not to attempt to get their partner to agree with their own perceptions. Empathetic understanding is the goal, not agreement! The speaker is encouraged to express the feelings experienced while making the drawing and the feelings experienced during the verbal sharing. The listener is encouraged to express feelings aroused by the partner's drawing and the verbal explanation of it. When the process is completed, roles are reversed and the process is repeated. The sharing of the two drawings usually takes about fifteen minutes, after which the total group discusses the value of the experience for about five minutes.

Participant couples frequently report a sense of closeness that comes from the renewed realization that they share a common history. Many are surprised that their drawing and that of their partner are quite similar. Others are surprised by the differences in perceptions that are expressed by the drawings and the verbal explanation of them. Emotional intimacy also frequently is experienced as happy and even sad feelings associated with historical events are remembered and shared.

LIFE-TIME DRAWING

Objectives: The objectives of the Life-Time Drawing experience are to identify and share perceptions of time usage for self and partner, to increase the ability to accurately and empathetically listen to each other and to share with another person of the opposite gender, expanding the boundaries of sharing, reducing our societally scripted sense of privatism, and raising the question of intimacy and friendship with persons of the opposite gender.

Time: Fifty-five minutes.

Procedure: Everyone is instructed to draw on a sheet of paper in their notebook their perception of how they actually use their time in an average week (168 hours). There is no restriction placed on the number or kind of categories the individual may use. Some common categories are eating, sleeping, work, housework, alone time, hobby time, recreational or sport time, time with the children, schoolwork, play, family time, time alone with spouse, time with relatives, community activities, sexual relationships, and so on. The drawing may be done in a pie form, varying the size of the slices, in graph form, or any other creative way the person chooses. When she or he has completed the drawing for self, a similar drawing is to be made on the reverse side of the paper showing how the individual perceives his partner's use of time. The kind of drawing (i.e., pie, graph) should be the same for both drawings. The giving of instructions, along with a sample drawing on newsprint, and the making of the two drawings usually takes about twenty minutes.

For the next fifteen minutes, each person shares his life-time drawing with someone else's partner (opposite gender). The listener's task is to encourage the speaker to be clear and specific in his description. After one has described the two drawings, roles are reversed and the process is repeated. During the final twenty minutes, marital partners discuss their drawings together. First, one presents both drawings, each being discussed in turn. Then, roles are reversed and the process is repeated.

BODY SHOP

Objectives: The objectives of the Body Shop exercise are to relieve tired sitting muscles and increase the flow of oxygen in the body, and to involve the body (and not just the mind) in the enrichment process, emphasizing and modeling the unity of the person.

Time: Ten minutes.

Procedure: Following a brief coffee break (ten minutes), a variety of body awareness activities can be used in this time period, including any of those described previously (e.g., body slapping, stretching, flopping, circle massage, etc.).

DISCUSSION: CIRCLE OF TRUST/DISTRUST

Objectives: The objectives of the Circle of Trust discussion are to place theoretical and cognitive underpinnings beneath the enrichment experience, and to affirm the importance of self-disclosure, risk, and acceptance in the building of a trusting relationship.

Time: Ten minutes.

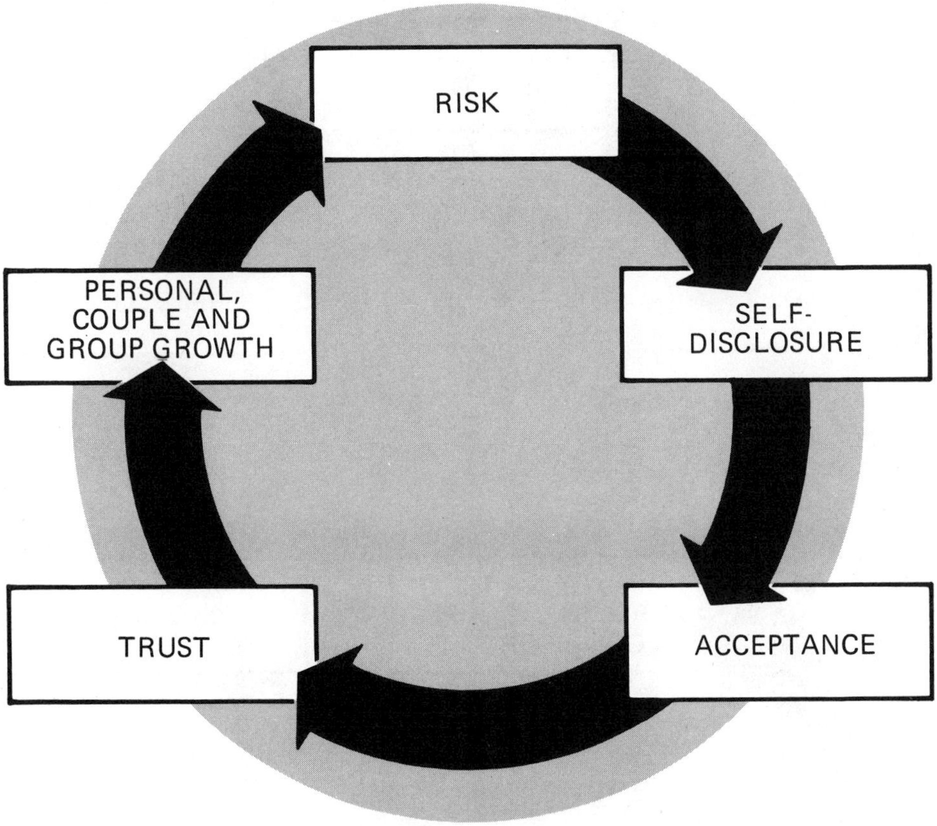

Figure 7.2. *Circle of Trust*

Procedure: In a lecture format, the following material is presented, preferably with personal illustrations by the leadership couple. In any relationship or group, appropriate risk, openness, acceptance, and trust are crucial elements in developing an atmosphere conducive to personal, couple and group growth. The responsibility for the formation of that atmosphere rests with each and every member of the couple or group. If I risk self-disclosure of my thoughts, feelings, or behaviors with you, and you accept that self-disclosure (not necessarily agree with it) as a valid expression and gift of myself, a bond of trust can be formed between us. That trust becomes the foundation on which personal, couple or group growth can be built. This, in turn, encourages further risk-taking and self-disclosure, and the circle of trust continues.

However, if I risk self-disclosure of my thoughts, feelings, or behaviors with you, and you reject that self-disclosure (e.g., "How can you possibly feel that way?"), distrust emerges between us (i.e., "It is not safe to disclose

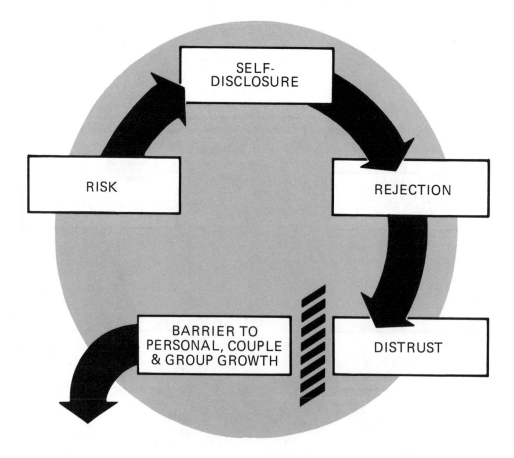

Figure 7.3. *Circle of Distrust*

things to you that leave me feeling vulnerable"), and a barrier to personal, couple and group growth is erected.

If this paradigm is truly reflective of what happens in a relationship or group, it is obvious that I must risk self-disclosure and so must you, to some extent. In addition, we must accept what each other has to say and disclose, not necessarily agree with it, but accept it as a gift of one person to another in the relationship or group. When this occurs on an ongoing basis, trust is formed and the opportunity is present for personal, relationship and group growth.

The giving of personal illustrations regarding the circle of trust/distrust by the leadership couple or team serves as an effective prelude to the My World of Feelings experience.

MY WORLD OF FEELINGS

Objectives: The objectives of the My World of Feelings experience are to increase the ability to experience and identify feelings in one's self, and to increase the ability to express feelings, and to hear and accept the feelings of one's spouse.

Time: Seventy-five minutes.

Procedure: The three-part My World of Feelings form (see the end of this section) is distributed to each participant. Part one is an overview of the experience, with suggested time parameters. Part two is a brief reading which focuses on the concept of feelings and their expression. Part three is a series of incomplete sentences designed to elicit feelings and facilitate their expression between partners as they are completed and shared.

Before the couples begin the experience, brief instructions are given, along with some comments and personal examples regarding the important place feelings have in relationships (approximately five minutes). The importance of individuals being aware of all kinds of feelings, accepting them in themselves, and being able to appropriately communicate and accept them in an effective relationship is stressed. It is also emphasized that feelings do not have to be justified or apologized for, and that the sharing of them is a gift of the self to another person, which, if accepted, can pave the way for stronger bonds of trust and deeper intimacy between persons.

Participants are instructed to find a place where they can be alone as a couple. Each person is to read silently The World of Feelings. When that has been accomplished, each individual completes in writing the sentences on the My World of Feelings form. When both partners have completed the sentences, they are to sit facing each other, perhaps knees touching, side-by-side, maintaining eye contact as much as possible throughout the experience. After deciding who will start, the one partner says, "In our marriage, when we relate together, I am happiest when . . .," and completes the statement. The listener is to listen attentively to the feelings being expressed, and to try to accept them. The only comment permitted by the listener is a question for clarification of what the speaker means. Statements are not to be discussed at this point or disagreed with. It is hoped that they will be heard, accepted, and received as a gift of the one person to the other. After the first person has expressed his response to the first item, the partner shares his response to the same item. The process is repeated until all seventeen statements have been verbally expressed by each partner, which usually takes about twenty minutes.

Couples are also instructed to spend at least ten minutes talking together about what they experienced, thought, and felt as they read the material, completed the sentences, and expressed them to each other. In addition, they are to discuss the value of this experience for them as individuals and for their relationship. This discussion as a couple is followed by a ten minute, total group discussion regarding the value of this experience and the value of the awareness, expression, and acceptance of feelings in relationships.

My World of Feelings Experience

15 minutes	1. Personal reading: "The World of Feelings"
15 minutes	2. Individuals complete statements on "My World of Feelings" form.
20 minutes	3. Couples sit facing each other, knees touching side-by-side; decide who will start.
	4. The person starting says, "In our marriage, when we relate together, I am happiest when . . . .," and completes the statement, maintaining eye contact as much as possible.
	5. Partner is to listen attentively to the feelings being expressed, and to accept them. The only comment acceptable is a question for clarification of what the person means. Statements are not to be discussed or disagreed with. They should be heard, accepted, and received as a gift of the one person to the other.
	6. After the first person has shared her/his response to item number 1, the partner

	then shares her/his response to the same item.
	7. The process is repeated until all the items have been completed.
10 minutes	8. Talk together with your partner about what you experienced, thought and felt as you went through this experience. Discuss the value of this experience for you and for your relationship.
10 minutes	9. When all couples have completed the process, there will be a brief period of total group sharing regarding the value of this experience.

70 minutes, total

The World of Feelings

The world of feelings is the world of affection and sentiment, the world of emotion and passion. It is the world of happiness and sadness, of joy and anger, of excitement and boredom. My feelings are my spontaneous emotional responses to the events that occur in the world around me, and the emotional responses associated with, and triggered by, my fulfilled or unfulfilled expectations and my interpretations of events and behaviors. My feelings are expressed in and through my body: I may get a knot in my stomach when I am anxious, or my palms may sweat; I may speak faster and louder when I am excited, and slower and softer when I am sad; my body may shake when I laugh, and my eyes may fill with tears when I am in pain. Even when I am not consciously aware of my feelings, my body is frequently giving off clues that I am feeling something, clues that other people may sense.

During any given day, I will feel a variety of feelings:

happiness	confusion	relief	satisfaction
sadness	loneliness	hope	boredom
joy	apathy	fear	love
pain	anger	confidence	suspense
suspicion	remorse	silliness	contentment
pride	irritation	peacefulness	tiredness
hopelessness	anticipation	reverence	surprise

The list could be expanded almost endlessly, with subtle variations and differing degrees of each feeling being present at different times. I can feel several feelings at once, and those feelings can conflict with each other.

My feelings are a very real and valuable part of me. They are just as important as my thoughts, my senses, and my behaviors. They can help me to deepen my understanding of life and the impact of people and events upon me. My joy helps me to celebrate and to identify things and people I like. My boredom gives me clues that I would rather be doing something else. My fears help me to protect myself. Without my feelings, I would live a greatly impoverished life.

Yet, for some reason, many of us have been taught to disregard our feelings—all of them, or a select few negative feelings. Some people have been taught to be rational. Some have been taught to deny or avoid anger, pain, pride, or sexual feelings. Perhaps, each of us has a little list inside us of acceptable and unacceptable feelings. Some of us have been taught so well that we don't even feel certain feelings. Others of us feel them internally, but we don't permit ourselves to express them with our words or actions. For example, we want to avoid conflict, so we don't express our anger. We don't want to be soft, so we withhold our warmth. We don't want to appear weak, so we don't disclose our fears.

If my feelings are to serve me and help me make sense of life, I must be aware of them and their heights and depths, and be able to express them appropriately in words and actions. If I deny or avoid them, I lose the ability to control them and they can gain control of me. Then, they may emerge when I don't want them to, perhaps inappropriately. Or, they may literally eat a hole in my stomach or give me a pounding headache. In some way, I pay a great price when I refuse to let my feelings have an appropriate and natural place in my life.

When I accept the fact that it is normal to feel a whole range of feelings, I am freed from justifying my feelings or apologizing for them. I simply recognize that, "I am human; therefore, I feel. You are human; therefore, you feel, too." As I accept that fact, and increase my awareness of my feelings, I can express them in many ways. The choice of how I will express them is mine to make. I can learn new ways. I can change old ways of expressing them. The more I practice, the more I will become used to expressing my feelings.

In a marital relationship, the ability of two individuals to be aware of the whole range of feelings, to express them appropriately, and to accept them in themselves and in each other, can pave the way for increased self-awareness, and for stronger bonds of trust and deeper intimacy. It may make each partner more vulnerable, too. But, perhaps the potential for self awareness and growth, and for increased trust and intimacy, is worth the risk!

My World of Feelings

Please complete the following statements:

1. In our marriage, when we relate together, I am happiest when . . .
2. In our marriage, when we relate together, I am saddest when . . .
3. In our marriage, when we relate together, I am angriest when . . .
4. The best thing about our marriage is . . .
5. I feel most afraid when . . .
6. I feel loved when you . . .
7. I feel appreciated when you . . .
8. My greatest concern/fear for our marriage is . . .
9. What I like most about myself is . . .
10. What I dislike most about myself is . . .
11. What I like most about you is . . .
12. My greatest concern/fear for you is . . .
13. The feelings that I have the most difficulty sharing with you are . . .
14. The feelings that I can share most easily with you are . . .
15. Right now I feel . . . towards you.
16. Right now I feel . . . towards myself.
17. I feel . . . sharing these feelings with you.

WANTS, NEEDS, AND FEARS LISTING

Objectives: The objectives of the Wants, Needs, and Fears Listing experience are to identify and express specific, personal wants, needs, and fears in the marriage relationship, and to begin the process of planning for change in the relationship.

Time: Fifty minutes.

Procedure: For the first five minutes, instructions and brief definitions of want, need, and fear are given. For the purpose of this experience, a *want* is defined as something earnestly desired in or from the marital relationship, but which is not defined by the individual as absolutely necessary for emotional survival in the relationship (e.g., "I want to spend more time with you on weekends"). With a want there is some implication of a willingness to negotiate for resolution of the issue. A *need* is defined as something which is essential and absolutely necessary in or from the marital relationship, and which is defined by the individual as necessary for continued emotional (sometimes even physical) survival in the relationship (e.g., "I need to have a continuing sense that you love me and value me"). The means by which the need is to be met may be negotiable, but the fulfillment of the need is deemed essential. A *fear* is defined as a sense of anxious concern or perceived danger regarding some aspect of the marital relationship (e.g., "I am afraid that if I push for the renegotiation of some of our marital roles, you will get so angry with me that I will withdraw. If I do that, I am afraid that I will harbor continuing resentments and we will lose some of our intimacy"). The listing of fears is included in this experience because we assume that unexpressed and unresolved fears frequently block the expression and successful meeting of perceived wants and needs.

For the next fifteen minutes, each individual is instructed to make three columns on a piece of paper in the spiral notebook, one each for wants, needs, and fears. Each person then creates a list of specific and personal wants, needs, and fears in the marriage relationship. The wants and needs lists should include those that currently are being met or fulfilled, as well as those that are not being met or fulfilled, or are only partially satisfied (e.g., "I need to know that you love me, and I get a sense each day that you do"—a need that is expressed and is currently being satisfactorily fulfilled).

After the list has been completed, each person is given an additional ten minutes to identify and list at least one specific thing she or he wants to be different regarding a want, need, or fear (e.g., "I want us both to reschedule a portion of our weekends so that we can do something, like play tennis, together"). An indication is to be made regarding what specifically would need to occur (e.g., changes in behaviors, assumptions, etc.) for the desired change to be implemented, and what the writer is specifically willing to do to implement the change.

For the last twenty minutes, partners share their respective lists, followed by the specific thing each wants to be different. At this point, agreement is not sought, nor is commitment to change requested. Expression of wants, needs, and fears and empathic understanding (total listening) are the desired end points.

DISCUSSIONS: HOW PEOPLE CHANGE; CONTRACTING

Objectives: The objectives of the How People Change and Contracting discussions are to increase understanding of the dynamics of change, and the need for risking new behaviors and for ongoing support if change is to become firmly integrated, and to understand the process of noncontingency contracting as one way of planning for and implementing change in a relationship.

Time: Twenty minutes.

Procedure: Two brief discussions are given to pave the way for the next experience, Contract Writing. Change is described as inevitable. Relationships will change. They do not remain static. People will change. They do not remain static. But, we do not have to wait for change to occur to us. We do not have to be victims of change. Instead, we can be agents of change for our personal lives and for our relationships. We can be actively involved in sensing the need or desire for change, in identifying specific, desired areas for change, in planning for change to occur, and in implementing the agreed upon plans. The choice of being a victim of change or an agent of change is ours to make. If we choose to be agents, we need to understand the dynamics of change, and to realize that effective, integrated change does not occur solely by chance. We need to want to change enough to plan for it, to develop necessary skills, and to work at it with discipline, patience and hope.

People change when the pain is too great for them to continue in the present pattern of behavior, when they are too bored to continue the way they are going, or, when they realize they can change. When the pain, boredom or realization that change is possible is of sufficient strength, the person must risk a change in behavior. This requires support from one's self, from others, and from one's value or religious system as the change takes place. Continued support is needed as the changed behavior continues if the new behavior is to become an integrated part of the person's life.

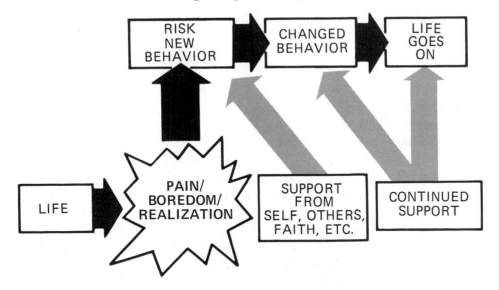

Figure 7.4. *Dynamics of Change*

If the support does not continue, the individual may regress to the prior behavior, or to an even more primitive level. The inability to successfully integrate a desired change in behavior is frequently accompanied with a sense of guilt and failure as a person. Whereas, the successful integration of new, desired behavior frequently leads to, and contributes to, increased self-esteem and increased interpersonal effectiveness. (With religiously oriented groups, appropriate scriptural references may provide an additional supportive framework to increase understanding of the possibility of change and the need for support, e.g., II Corinthians 5:17, 1:3–4.)

The discussion on the dynamics of change is immediately followed by a discussion on Contracting. A noncontingent contract is suggested as a potentially helpful instrument and process that involves a commitment to one's self or to someone else to make a desired change. It does not require that someone else do something in return (a *quid pro quo* contract). According to James and Jongeward (1971), a contract must be "clear, concise, and direct. It involves a decision to do something about a specific problem, a statement of a clear goal to be worked toward in language simple enough for . . . [all parties] to understand, and the possibility of the goal's being fulfilled" (pp. 231–232).

Such a contract should be: written; specific; achievable; time-oriented—that is, contain a specific date by which the contract is to be fulfilled; signed by all parties involved; and posted in a conspicuous place so that it can serve as a visual reminder to all parties involved. An example is: "For the next three Saturday afternoons, we will play tennis together from 2:00 to 4:00."

CONTRACT WRITING

Objective: The objective of the Contract Writing experience is to develop the ability to plan for specific change in the marital relationship using a contracting process.

Time: Thirty-five minutes.

Procedure: Couples are instructed to decide upon an area in which they would like to make a contract for change. The lists from the Wants, Needs, and Fears experience frequently provide helpful information for the identification of an area in which change is needed and possible. After the area has been identified, each person reflects upon, and expresses, his or her wants, needs, and fears in that area. The couple indicates at least one specific thing they want to be different in their relationship with regard to the identified area. They decide what would need to happen for that desired change to occur, and each person expresses what she or he is willing to do to facilitate the change.

The couple is then to agree on and write a specific, achievable, time-oriented contract to change one aspect of their relationship. They are to include a date by which the contract will be completed. It is to be signed by both parties, and "sealed with a kiss" or other nonverbal expression of caring.

Contracts vary greatly, and no standard is to be set. Whatever each couple identifies as meaningful for them is appropriate. For example, one couple may contract to play tennis together once a week for four weeks.

Another couple may develop a unilateral contract in which the husband assumes responsibility to arrange his schedule to have at least two evening meals per week, for one month, with his family. Another couple may contract for separate time, time away from each other for the next two weeks. The possibilities are virtually endless.

During the thirty-five minute time period, many couples are able to complete several contracts. When the total group re-forms, the opportunity is given for couples to verbally express their contracts. To conclude the experience, personal commitment and responsibility are emphasized and the couples are encouraged to post the contracts at home (to serve as a reminder), to review them periodically, and to continue to practice the process of planning, writing and implementing contracts for change.

INDIVIDUAL AND MARRIAGE STRENGTHS LISTING

Objectives: The objectives of the Individual and Marriage Strengths Listing experience are to increase the ability to identify and verbally affirm individual and marital strengths, and to increase the sense of self-worth and couple bonding, through the process of strength bombardment.

Time: One hundred minutes.

Procedure: For the first five minutes, couples receive instructions for the experience. Because of the many steps involved in this exercise, it is crucial that couples be able to also see the instructions posted on newsprint and have continued reference to them during the exercise.

Each couple decides which partner will be focused upon first. The focus person lists his personal strengths (e.g., what I do effectively, good health, easy-going personality, warmth, ability to say "No," etc.) and potential strengths (i.e., strengths that are in the process of emerging or of being enhanced, e.g., developing the ability to listen more effectively and express feelings directly). At the same time that the focus person is creating his list, the partner is creating a similar list of what he or she believes are the strengths and potential strengths of the focus person.

When both lists are completed, the focus person shares his list with the partner. When that is done, the focus person specifically asks the partner to share his list. (The purpose for specifically requesting positive feedback is to force participants to face our societal prohibition against seeking direct, positive affirmation of ourselves.) The partner then expresses his perceptions, giving specific examples where helpful or desired. Throughout the experience, each person may feel free to ask questions for clarification, but may not openly disagree with perceptions of individual strengths and potential strengths. When both lists have been completely shared, the initial listener asks the focus person how he felt during the experience and what is being felt at that particular moment. After the focus person has responded, roles are reversed, and the process is repeated. Our experience has been that it takes approximately twenty minutes per person to accomplish the Individual Strength Listing phase of the experience.

The total group is reassembled, and for the next fifteen minutes each person is given the opportunity to move to a designated spot and say, "My name is . . . (first and last name), and one neat, great and wonderful thing about me is . . ." Each person who desires to participate is free to complete the statement any way he or she desires. We have heard statements from, "My name is Mary Smith, and one neat, great and wonderful thing about me is that I am a caring person," to "My name is John Doe and one neat, great and wonderful thing about me is that I had the guts to get up here and say this." As people express themselves, spontaneous applause frequently emerges, as the group gets caught-up in the positiveness of the experience. After all of those have participated who desired to do so, the total group discusses the experience and the feelings they were aware of during the exercise.

An alternative to the above is for each person or couple to get together with another person or couple to share the individual strengths lists. After each person has shared his list, the participants discuss the question, "How did you feel sharing with other people and telling them your strengths?" The total group then briefly discusses the experience.

Many individuals report this to be the most difficult, yet one of the most rewarding, aspects of the entire program. To focus on oneself in a positive sense, to identify personal strengths and potential strengths, to express them in writing and verbally to one's partner, to request positive feedback from one's partner and receive it, and then to risk public affirmation of one's self, is frequently an overwhelming experience, in the positive sense. Parental and societal warnings against being self-centered or conceited are exposed, and, at least momentarily balanced with a message that it is appropriate to affirm oneself and to receive direct and positive affirmation. The positive support and affirmation from one's partner and from the group experience frequently contributes to the increased sense of self-esteem and well-being generated by the self-examination and self-affirmation.

For the next twenty-five minutes, each couple sits together and creates a joint list of marital strengths and potential strengths. When they have made as exhaustive a list as possible, they compare their list with Otto's "Outline of Marriage Strengths" (Otto, 1969) (see the end of this section), and expand their list if they discover strengths they have overlooked or omitted. They then discuss the implications of this experience for their marriage relationship, and identify the strengths they want to develop further. Contracts can be developed in subsequent weeks to develop those strengths or potential strengths.

Each couple gets together with one other couple, and the lists of marriage strengths are shared. Each partner of a couple is to express at least some of the strengths, to prevent one partner from dominating the interchange. When the lists have been shared, the four people discuss their feelings about sharing their marital strengths in a small group. This phase of the experience usually takes about ten minutes, and is followed by a brief, five-minute, total group discussion of the value of focusing upon and expressing individual and marriage strengths and potential strengths.

Outline of Marriage Strengths

Using traditions and rituals in your marriage: observing birthdays, anniversaries, holidays, special days.

Participating in community, local and national issues: attending functions together, participating in organizations, becoming involved in selected issues and concerns.

Fostering curiosity, interest and creativity in each other: sharing interests, reading material, encouraging creative expression, encouraging the elements of surprise and spontaneity, trying new things, developing and doing something special and exciting together.

Sharing recreational and educational needs: enjoying fun, play, games, sports, recreation together; enjoying educational experiences, encouraging each other educationally.

Meeting emotional needs: sensitivity to needs for warmth, affection, love and understanding; the presence of acceptance, caring, trust, affection, affirmation and celebration in the marriage.

Mutual satisfaction from sexual relations: enjoying love-making together, the element of celebration in sex.

Having and enjoying friends (and relatives) together and separately: accepting and recognizing that friends and relatives can be enjoyed either together or separately, having close friends who are positive for you and your marriage.

Open communication: being honest and leveling with each other; talking things out, sharing feelings and thoughts; working things through honestly and openly.

Sharing spiritual life: ability to talk over and share deep and moving experiences together; having deep and meaningful and celebrative experiences together; experiencing something special that is deep and spiritual and religious.

Giving encouragement to each other: giving encouragement and support in daily work, chores, responsibilities, and in other areas; the presence of affirmation, caring, support and encouragement in the marriage.

Organizational ability: ability to organize and do things together for greater efficiency; ability to plan and to carry it out.

Ability to do things together, flexibility: husband can assume some of wife's functions and roles, and wife, some of husband's, as determined by needs and circumstances; the presence of flexibility, give-and-take, movement, change, growth, spontaneity.

DISCUSSION: INCLUSION, CONTROL AND AFFECTION

Objective: The objective of this discussion is to understand inclusion, control and affection as three dimensions of any relationship.

Time: Twenty-five minutes.

Procedure: In a lecture format in which questions and comments from the participants are encouraged, a brief overview of Schutz's (1966, 1971, 1973, 1978) theory of Inclusion, Control and Affection is presented.

According to William Schutz, all individuals have three basic interpersonal needs which manifest in various behaviors and feelings in the individual's relationships with other people. These three basic needs—inclusion, control and affection—are based upon the individual's perception of, and feelings about, himself or herself (Schutz, 1973). In terms of marital relationships, these three needs are suggested to be the ongoing basic concerns of the relationship.

"Inclusion refers to feelings about being important or significant, of having some worth, that people will care. Inclusion behavior refers to associations between people, being excluded or included, belonging, togetherness. The need to be included manifests as wanting to be attended to, and to attract attention and interaction" (Schutz, 1971, pp. 17–18). Some people have high inclusion needs, and seek to do everything in a group or with other people. Other people have low inclusion needs, and tend to be introverted and prefer to do many things alone. Overconcern with inclusion needs can lead to an individual's inability to be alone and to so-called "oversocial" behavior. Too little concern with inclusion needs can lead to severe introversion and social isolation, so-called "undersocial" behavior. The basic concern in the area of inclusion is *in* or *out.*

Control refers to "the feeling of competence, including intelligence, appearance, practicality, and general ability to cope with the world" (Schutz, 1971, p. 17). "Control behavior refers to the decision-making process between people and the areas of power, influence and authority. The need for control varies along a continuum from the desire for authority over others (and therefore over one's future), to the need to be controlled and have responsibility lifted from the self" (Schutz, 1971, p. 24). The basic concern in the area of control is *top* or *bottom.*

"The area of affection revolves around feelings of being lovable, of feeling that if one's personal core is revealed in its entirety it will be seen as a lovely thing" (Schutz, 1971, p. 17). "Affection behavior refers to close personal emotional feelings between two people, especially love and hate in their various degrees" (Schutz, 1971, p. 27). Too much of a concern with affection needs can lead to the so-called "overpersonal" individual who appears to overflow with feelings in whatever situation he or she is involved, and who attempts to get very close to other people as quickly as possible. Too little of a concern with affection needs can lead to so-called "underpersonal" behavior, or the inability or lack of desire to be involved in close, feeling-relationships. The basic concern in the area of affection is *close* or *far*.

"In the inclusion phase of a relationship, people must *encounter* each other and decide to continue their relation; control issues require them to confront one another and work out how they will be related" (Schutz, 1971, p. 28). They must work out the means by which the relationship will be continued with regard to power, authority, and so on. In order for the relationship to continue, the individuals need to form ties of affection and embrace each other, literally or figuratively, to form a lasting bond and also to be able to part ways (Schutz, 1971).

Although inclusion needs tend to be especially addressed when a relationship is being formed, those needs must also continue to be addressed as a relationship continues to grow and develop. So must control and affection needs continue to be addressed. The three needs are interdependent and overlap each other, and are continually being addressed, even simultaneously, in any given relationship.

In order for a relationship to be mutually satisfying, the persons involved in it must come to grips with these issues of inclusion, control and affection and resolve them in ways they find appropriate and meaningful. In individuals and relationships, which are in a constant state of development, these needs have differing levels of intensity and urgency at different points in time. At one point in the individual or relationship life cycle, inclusion needs may be in the foreground. At another point, intimacy or affection needs may require the most attention. Therefore, any resolution of these issues needs to be viewed as immediate, dynamic, and subject to change as the individual and relationship needs change and develop over time, rather than as rigid or inflexible.

Each individual must, therefore, develop an appropriate and satisfying balance in his life with regard to these needs of inclusion, control and affection. To do that effectively within the context of a marital relationship requires self-awareness and self-esteem as well as awareness of, and esteem for, the other person in the relationship. Differences between one's own needs and desires, as well as differences between partners, lead to inevitable internal and interpersonal conflicts. These differences need to be addressed openly and directly in order for satisfying dynamic solutions to be achieved. In order for that to occur, individuals and couples must be encouraged and enabled to explore all three of the areas of interpersonal need. They also need to be encouraged to acquire skills that will facilitate the development of an appropriate and satisfying balance, and, through that balance, a fulfilling marital relationship. The achievement of that goal is the ultimate aim of the Creative Marriage Enrichment Program.

This theory is one of the key foundation stones of our program. Up to this point, the focus has been upon the area of inclusion needs. The focus will now shift to the area of control needs, and then to the area of affection.

GROUP CIRCLE AND HUG

Objective: The objective of the Group Circle and Hug experience is to develop a sense of "we-ness" in the group which includes the potential for touch.

Time: Five minutes.

Procedure: The participants are requested to form a circle with arms around each other's waists, and to look around the circle, making eye contact with as many people as possible. The group then moves as close together as possible, with each person hugging the person on each side, in effect creating a group hug. Arms are dropped, and the group is dismissed. (With religiously oriented groups, voluntary, individual, verbal sentence prayers—with open or closed eyes—frequently add a dimension of spiritual intimacy to the group's life, contributing to the development of a common bond in the group.) If the program is being conducted over a weekend, this experience completes the section on inclusion needs and closes Saturday evening.

8

The Creative Marriage Enrichment Program: Control

William Schutz has defined the interpersonal need for *control* as "the need to establish and maintain a satisfactory relationship with people with respect to control and power. Control behavior refers to the decision-making process between people. Some terms that connote aspects of primarily positive control are, 'power, authority, dominance, influence, control, ruler, superior, officer, leader' " (Schutz, 1978, p. 8). Effective resolution of the interpersonal need for control includes the ability to negotiate role expectations and to use conflict creatively. The second major emphasis of the Creative Marriage Enrichment Program is this interpersonal need for control.

The exercises are presented as if the decision has been made to conduct the program over a weekend, from Friday evening to Sunday evening. This phase of the program would begin on Sunday morning. The direct focus on the interpersonal need for control follows a brief series of Wake-Up Exercises and a "Where Are You?" experience designed to help participant couples to express their response to the program to this point in time and their expectations for the remainder of the weekend.

WAKE-UP EXERCISES

Objectives: The objectives of the Wake-Up Exercises are the following: to "wake-up" the body, and increase alertness, by stimulating body muscles and increasing the blood flow to all parts of the body; to involve the body (and not just the mind) in the enrichment process, emphasizing and modeling the unity of the person.

Time: Fifteen minutes.

Procedure: A variety of body awareness activities can be used in this time period, including the stretching, slapping and flopping exercises described earlier. In addition, participants can share some of the exercises that they find helpful and invigorating. Those who are willing can take turns leading the group through one or more of their favorite exercises.

"WHERE ARE YOU?"

Objectives: The objectives of the "Where Are You?" experience are to review the goals established at the beginning of the program and reflect upon the progress made (or not made) towards fulfilling them, to reaffirm those goals or create new ones for the remainder of the program, and to increase the ability to share with other people (reducing privatism) and develop a sense of a supportive community.

Time: Twenty minutes.

Procedure: Each couple is instructed to meet with one other couple. The four people are to share briefly their opinions, thoughts and feelings regarding the program to this point, its effect upon them as individuals and as a couple, and what they expect to happen, hope will happen, or fear will happen today. They are to review their individual and marital goals for the weekend, reflect briefly upon the progress made (or not made) towards fulfilling them, and then to reaffirm those goals or generate new ones for the remainder of the program. After each person has had the opportunity to express himself, the total group meets and participants are given the opportunity to verbalize expectations, hopes, fears, and "where they are" as the emphasis on the interpersonal need for control begins.

Individuals and couples frequently express a sense of renewed closeness at this point in the program. Different experiences (e.g., Communication Skills, Marriage Life Line, My World of Feelings, Contract Writing, and Individual and Marriage Strengths Listing), as well as the whole positive emphasis of the program and the setting, are referred to as significant triggers for that closeness. In addition, some apprehension is usually expressed regarding the upcoming focus on marital roles and conflict. This is to be expected, because the issue of marital roles is such a live one in contemporary American society, and many couples are aware of significant differences in that area between partners. At the same time, many individuals and couples have not been appropriately trained to cope with the conflict generated by those differences. In fact, many have been taught that conflict is bad or wrong. In short, there are significant deficits in social learning regarding the management and utilization of conflict. Therefore, apprehension and anxiety are to be expected, as conflict laden issues are approached.

MARITAL ROLE EXPECTATIONS

Objectives: The objectives of the Marital Role Expectations experience are to identify, express and learn to negotiate or renegotiate role expectations, and to increase the ability to cope creatively with conflict.

Time: Seventy-five minutes.

Procedure: For the first ten minutes, participants are instructed how to complete the Marital Role Sheets (based on Hurvitz, 1961). Each participant receives a sheet headed "Female," and one headed "Male." Each person is to fill out the sheet for the male or the female, whichever gender the leadership couple or team arbitrarily decides to focus on first.

Marital Role Sheet

Female

DECISION MAKER

Wife makes the final decision when the family is unable to agree.

_____ WP*   _____ HE†

FEMALE MODEL

Wife serves as a female model for family members, demonstrating appropriate behaviors, attitudes and feelings as a woman, wife, and mother. She expresses these by the way she performs her other roles.

_____ WP   _____ HE

SPIRITUAL OR PHILOSOPHICAL LEADER

Wife is a spiritual or philosophical leader in the home, expressing and practicing religious beliefs, a value stance, or philosophical attitude toward life and the world.

_____ WP   _____ HE

HOUSEHOLD WORKER

Wife does her work around the house.

_____ WP   _____ HE

---

*WP = Wife's Priorities/Performance (What I *do* reflects my *priorities*.)

†HE = Husband's Expectations

MONEY MANAGER

Wife manages the family finances.

———— WP   ———— HE

SEX PARTNER

Wife is a sex partner to her husband. She understands her own and his sexual needs and responds to them in a mutually satisfactory way.

———— WP   ———— HE

COMPANION

Wife is a companion to her husband, sharing social and recreational activities, leisure time, thoughts, etc., with him. She regards him as a friend and confidante.

———— WP   ———— HE

HELPS HUSBAND

Wife helps husband with his work around the house when needed.

———— WP   ———— HE

SOURCE OF LOVE

Wife gives love, affection, understanding and support to her husband and other family members. She seeks fulfillment of herself as a person and she helps her husband fulfill himself.

———— WP   ———— HE

MOTHER

Wife helps the children grow by being a mother to them. She involves herself appropriately in their experiences and feelings as a friendly and concerned adult.

———— WP   ———— HE

BREADWINNER

Wife earns, or helps earn, the family's resources.

———— WP   ———— HE

COMMUNITY REPRESENTATIVE

Wife accepts civic responsibilities, represents the family in the community, and is involved in community groups, projects, etc.

———— WP   ———— HE

HOSTESS	CO-WORKER
Wife serves as a hostess to entertain friends and associates.	Wife shares household responsibilities with her husband (i.e., mutual responsibility, as opposed to "her work" and "his work.")

_____ WP   _____ HE   _____ WP   _____ HE

Marital Role Sheet

Male

DECISION MAKER

Husband makes the final decision when the family is unable to agree.

_____ HP*   _____ WE†

MALE MODEL

Husband serves as a male model for family members, demonstrating appropriate behaviors, attitudes and feelings as a man, husband, and father. He expresses these by the way he performs his other roles.

_____ HP   _____ WE

SPIRITUAL OR PHILOSOPHICAL LEADER

Husband is a spiritual or philosophical leader in the home, expressing and practicing religious beliefs, a value stance, or philosophical attitude toward life and the world.

_____ HP   _____ WE

HOUSEHOLD WORKER

Husband does his work around the house.

_____ HP   _____ WE

MONEY MANAGER

Husband manages the family finances.

_____ HP   _____ WE

SEX PARTNER

Husband is a sex partner to his wife. He understands his own and her sexual needs and responds to them in a mutually satisfactory way.

_____ HP   _____ WE

---

*HP = Husband's Priorities/Performance (What I *do* reflects my *priorities.*)

†WE = Wife's Expectations

COMPANION

Husband is a companion to his wife, sharing social and recreational activities, leisure time, thoughts, etc., with her. He regards her as a friend and confidante.

_____ HP   _____ WE

HELPS WIFE

Husband helps wife with her work around the house when needed.

_____ HP   _____ WE

SOURCE OF LOVE

Husband gives love, affection, understanding and support to his wife and other family members. He seeks fulfillment of himself as a person and he helps his wife fulfill herself.

_____ HP   _____ WE

FATHER

Husband helps the children grow by being a father to them. He involves himself appropriately in their experiences and feelings as a friendly and concerned adult.

_____ HP   _____ WE

BREADWINNER

Husband earns, or helps earn, the family's financial resources.

_____ HP   _____ WE

COMMUNITY REPRESENTATIVE

Husband accepts civic responsibilities, represents the family in the community, and is involved in community groups, projects, etc.

_____ HP   _____ WE

HOST

Husband serves as a host to entertain friends and associates.

_____ HP   _____ WE

CO-WORKER

Husband shares household responsibilities with his wife (i.e., mutual responsibility, as opposed to "his work" and "her work.")

_____ HP   _____ WE

Individuals read the fourteen roles described on the Marital Role Sheet currently under consideration. (For illustrative purposes, we will assume that the decision has been made to focus on the Female Marital Role Sheet first.) The wife is to rank order, from one to fourteen, her priorities of the roles described. For example, if she believed "Source of Love" was her first priority, she would place a number one in the space labelled WP (Wife's Priority) under that role description. If she believed "Community Representative" was her fourteenth priority, she would place a number fourteen in the space labelled WP under that role description. Participants are requested to use all numbers, from one to fourteen, and not to give several roles a number 1 marking, several a middle ranking of 7, and several a low ranking of 14. A forced choice is requested.

Participants sometimes ask what we mean by priority. They wonder if it is what they really value or are forced to do by circumstances, indicating that there may be a significant difference between actual behaviors and internal values. For the purpose of this exercise, we suggest that the focus be upon actual performance, what ones does as opposed to what one believes or wishes were true. Participants are instructed to carefully note perceived differences between behaviors and internal values and to openly discuss them during the period of time set aside for couple interaction. Resolution of such differences may pave the way for the development of a fully congruent value stance regarding those roles, a stance in which behaviors and wishes or internal values are fully reflective of each other and not at variance.

It is also emphasized that this is not an exhaustive list of marital roles, and that particular persons or couples may believe that some of the described roles do not apply to them. They may indicate this by giving such items very low priority numbers, and by sharing their reasoning during the discussion time with partners.

While the wife is completing her form, using the WP spaces, the husband is also to read the described roles on the Female Marital Role Sheet. He is to decide what his expectations are of his wife and to rank order his priorities of the roles described. For example, if he believed "Companion" was his first priority, that is, his primary expectation of his wife, he would place a number one in the space labelled HE (Husband's Expectations) under that role description. If he believed "Breadwinner" was his eighth priority, he would place a number eight in the space labelled HE under that role description. Here again, a forced choice from one to fourteen is requested.

When the Female Marital Role Sheet has been completed by the participants (approximately ten minutes) each individual completes the Male Marital Role Sheet, using the same procedure and guidelines just outlined (approximately ten minutes). When both sheets have been completed, the male receives the Male Marital Role Sheet completed by his partner. He, in turn gives her the Female Marital Role Sheet he has completed. To reduce the number of forms to be viewed, the wife transfers the numbers assigned to each role description by her husband (HE column) to the Female Marital Role Sheet she has completed. She places those numbers in the blank HE column on her sheet and discards his form. Her expressed priorities and his expressed expectations will thus be easily viewed, side by side. The husband performs a similar transfer of numbers from the Male Marital Role Sheet his wife completed (WE column) to the sheet he has completed for himself (using the blank WE column). The form the wife completed is then discarded. The transfer of assigned numbers usually takes less than five minutes.

Each couple is given a total of twenty minutes to discuss both sheets. They are instructed to focus on thoughts as well as feelings. Each has the opportunity to express what surprises they encountered, to explain why they ranked certain things as they did, and to express what changes they would like to see made. The leadership couple stresses that differences are to be expected, and that understanding is the initial goal. If each person can understand what the other person perceives, wishes, and is endeavoring to communicate, the possibilities for mutual affirmation, respect of differences, and successful negotiation of desired changes are greatly enhanced.

After the couples have completed their interchange, the total group meets for twenty minutes to discuss briefly the value of the experience and to hear the following discussion on role renegotiation. This discussion is based on the work of Sherwood and Glidewell (1973), and a diagram ("Role Renegotiation") presenting the material in a visual form is distributed to each participant.

A marital role is defined as "any expectation that a particular husband, wife, or couple are to fulfill within the marital relationship." These roles are learned and are strongly influenced by one's society and culture. They can be narrowly defined and rigid, based soley on gender, or they can be shared or flexible and modifiable over time, according to the emerging and changing needs and wishes of different individuals and couples.

Such roles can be established overtly or covertly, by open and explicit decision-making or by tacit agreement. In either case, there are certain clearly definable stages which are evident. The first stage can be labeled "Sharing Information and Negotiating Expectations." During this stage, each person communicates in some way his or her wants, wishes, expectations,

The original version of this figure was created and copyrighted © 1971 by John J. Sherwood, and is used here in adapted form with his permission. The adapted version appeared in "Minnesota Couples Communication Program," by E. W. Nunnally, S. Miller, and D.B. Wackman, in *Marriage and Family Enrichment: New Perspectives and Programs,* 1976, edited by H. A. Otto. It is used here by permission of the publishers, Abingdon Press.

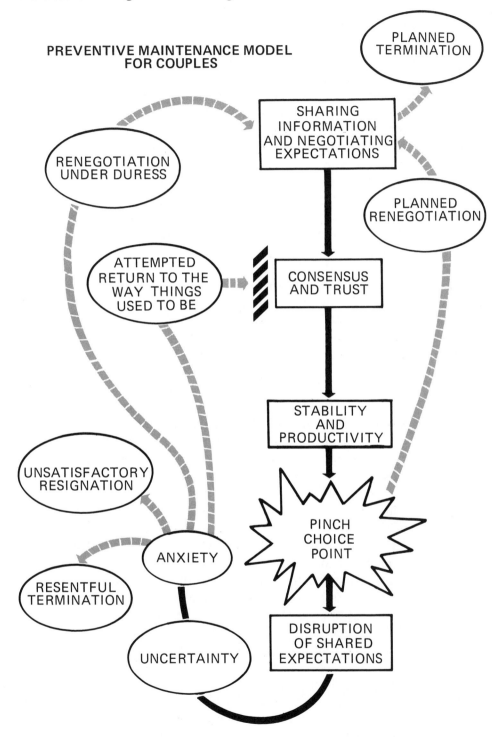

PREVENTIVE MAINTENANCE MODEL FOR COUPLES

PLANNED TERMINATION

SHARING INFORMATION AND NEGOTIATING EXPECTATIONS

RENEGOTIATION UNDER DURESS

PLANNED RENEGOTIATION

ATTEMPTED RETURN TO THE WAY THINGS USED TO BE

CONSENSUS AND TRUST

STABILITY AND PRODUCTIVITY

UNSATISFACTORY RESIGNATION

PINCH CHOICE POINT

ANXIETY

RESENTFUL TERMINATION

UNCERTAINTY

DISRUPTION OF SHARED EXPECTATIONS

Figure 8.1. *Role Renegotiation*

demands, and so on, regarding the role in question. Through a verbal or nonverbal process, a negotiated settlement is reached, agreement is made, and the couple moves to the second stage, which can be labeled "Commitment to the Role," or the period of "Consensus and Trust." During this stage, each person appropriately indicates, by word or actions and internal acceptance, that agreement on that particular role has been achieved. A period of "Stability and Productivity" follows, during which each person behaves in accordance with the agreed upon role, internally accepts the role as appropriate, and is content with the situation. Inevitably though, a period of "Disruption of Shared Expectations" emerges. We say inevitably, because people change over time as do their expectations of each other. In addition, some expectations and information (e.g., feelings) may have been withheld initially, either by conscious choice, or simply because the person was not aware of the thoughts or feelings at that time.

Since many people have been taught that conflict is bad or to be avoided at all costs, the emergence of the period of "Disruption of Shared Expectations" is frequently not highly valued. This can lead to the denial of emerging signs that something is wrong, the so-called "Pinch Choice Point." That point can be defined as a period of discomfort in which the realization begins to emerge that everything is not all right anymore, and one or both partners are dissatisfied with some aspect of a marital role.

If "Disruption of Shared Expectations" can be viewed as inevitable, and as an indicator of needed change, rather than as an indictment of a relationship or person, individuals and couples need not fear rocking the boat. Instead, they can be sensitive to the beginning phases of the stage of disruption, the pinch choice points. They can then express their feelings and perceptions, the need for role renegotiation, *before* deep feelings of hurt, anger and resentment accumulate, before blame is placed, and before the situation becomes so disruptive or destructive that good-will is threatened or destroyed.

When a destructive spiral has gained momentum, constructive change is extremely difficult and sometimes impossible to achieve. In such a situation, feelings of uncertainty and anxiety frequently abound, along with anger, pain and fear. Unsatisfactory resignation to living with things the way they are, an attempt to kiss and make-up and return to the way things used to be, forced renegotiation (i.e., "we'll reach a new agreement or else . . ."), and possibly even resentful termination of the relationship are all possible outcomes when pinch choice points are avoided or overlooked and a destructive spiral is permitted to gain momentum. However, careful attention to pinch choice points opens up the possibility for planned renegotiation of marital roles (and if necessary, planned termination of the relationship). If planned renegotiation is chosen, the process begins all over again, with the sharing of information and the negotiating of expectations.

The value upon which this theoretical model is built is clearly expressed and affirmed, namely, that marital roles need to be viewed as flexible and subject to change, according to the needs and wishes of different individuals and couples, rather than as stereotyped, rigid, inflexible, and unchanging over time. To dramatize this point and to conclude this experience, the following dramatic reading, "Playing Masculine/Playing Feminine" (Roszak and Roszak, 1969), is presented by the leadership couple or team.

"PLAYING MASCULINE/PLAYING FEMININE"*

Male: I am playing masculine.

Female: I am playing feminine.

Male: I am playing masculine because she is playing feminine.

Female: I am playing feminine because he is playing masculine.

Male: I am playing the kind of man that she thinks the kind of woman she is playing ought to admire.

Female: I am playing the kind of woman that he thinks the kind of man he is playing ought to desire.

Male: If I were not playing masculine, I might well be more feminine than she is—except when she is playing very feminine.

Female: If I were not playing feminine, I might well be more masculine than he is—except when he is playing very masculine.

Male: So I play harder . . .

Female: And I play . . . softer.

Male: I want to make sure that she could never be more masculine than I am.

Female: I want to make sure that he could never be more feminine than I am.

Male: I therefore seek to destroy the femininity in myself.

Female: I therefore seek to destroy the masculinity in myself.

Female: I am supposed to admire him for the masculinity in him that I fear in myself.

Male: I am supposed to desire her for the feminity in her that I despise in myself.

Male: I desire her for her femininity which is my femininity, but which I can never lay claim to.

Female: I admire him for his masculinity which is my masculinity, but which I can never lay claim to.

Male: Since I may only love my own femininity in her, I envy her her femininity.

Female: Since I may only love my own masculinity in him, I envy him his masculinity.

Unison: The envy poisons our love!

Male: I, coveting her unattainable femininity, decide to punish her.

Female: I, coveting his unattainable masculinity, decide to punish him.

Male: I denigrate her femininity—which I am supposed to desire and which I really envy, and I become more aggressively masculine.

Female: I feign disgust at his masculinity—which I am supposed to admire and which I really envy, and I become more fastidiously feminine.

————
        *Adapted from pages vii–viii in *Masculine/Feminine: Readings in Sexual Mythology and The Liberation of Women,* Edited by Betty Roszak and Theodore Roszak (Harper and Row, Harper Colophon edition) Copyright © 1969 by Betty Roszak and Theodore Roszak. Reprinted by permision of the publisher.

Male: I am becoming less and less what I want to be.
Female: I am becoming less and less what I want to be.
Male: But now I'm more manly than ever . . .
Female: And I am more womanly than ever.
Female: My femininity, growing more dependently supine, becomes contemptible.
Male: My masculinity, growing more oppressively domineering, becomes intolerable.
Female: At last, I loathe what I have helped his masculinity to become.
Male: At last, I loathe what I have helped her femininity to become.
Unison: So far, it has been very symmetrical. But we have left one thing out.
Male: The world belongs to what my masculinity has become. The reward for what my masculinity has become is power.
Female: The reward for what my femininity has become is only the security which his power can bestow on me.
Male: If I were to yield to what her femininity has become, I would be yielding to contemptible incompetence.
Female: If I were to acquire what his masculinity has become, I would participate in intolerable coerciveness.
Male: She is stifling under the triviality of her femininity . . .
Female: I am stifling under the triviality of my femininity.
Female: The world is groaning beneath the terrors of his masculinity.
Male: The world is groaning beneath the terrors of my masculinity.
Female: He is playing masculine.
Male: I am playing masculine.
Male: She is playing feminine.
Female: I am playing feminine.
Unison: How do we call off the game?

TOTAL GROUP CIRCLE MASSAGE

Objectives: The objectives of the Total Group Circle Massage are to relieve tired muscles, and to contribute to the building of a sense of community which includes the possibility of giving and receiving in a physical, nonsexual way.

Time: Five minutes.

Procedure: The participants are requested to form a tight circle and to turn to the right. Each person gently massages the shoulders, neck and back of the person in front of him or her. After a few minutes, each person does an about-face and repeats the process. After a few more minutes, participants are instructed to stretch the body in any way they find helpful, to relieve tired muscles and invigorate the body.

CONFLICT UTILIZATION

Objectives: The objectives of the Conflict Utilization experience are to develop or increase the ability to cope effectively with conflict, to learn one theoretical model for coping with conflict, providing a conceptual framework for times of crisis, and to develop a sense that conflict can be approached in a group setting and that supportive help can be received from group members (reducing "privatism").

Time: One hundred minutes.

Procedure: This experience begins with a ten minute discussion, "How To Have A Good Clean Fight." The steps are listed on newsprint and on a handout given to each participant. Conflict is described as inevitable between people who live in close proximity to each other and relate intimately on a variety of levels and issues. It is affirmed that it is not conflict *per se* that affects relationships, but how that conflict is approached, utilized, handled and resolved. If handled effectively, it can lead to greater intimacy. Effective resolution of conflict is defined as the creative use of differences. Seven steps for utilizing or managing conflict are described.

Step one. Listen to yourself. Identify and own your feelings to yourself and your partner (e.g., "I feel angry and hurt right now"). To "own" feelings means to accept them as one's own feelings, and not to blame one's partner for the way one feels. It is our belief that the angry and hurt feelings must be identified and expressed before effective and mutual problem solving can be accomplished (Mace, 1976; L'Abate, 1977b). However, the anger need not be expressed explosively (Ellis, 1976; Mace, 1976); and, the frequently underlying fears and hurt feelings must also be exposed and expressed. This requires a willingness to become vulnerable to one's partner.

Step two. Identify the real issue which is frequently not the issue originally presented. For example, beneath the statement, "I am angry that you don't spend enough time with the children," may be another issue, "I feel overwhelmed by my responsibilities with the children and abandoned by you, and I want and need some direct support and help from you." Immediate problem solving regarding "more time with the children" by the one partner would not necessarily lead to the exposing of the feelings and the issue of the other partner's feeling overwhelmed and abandoned.

Step three. Stay here and now. In other words, don't drag up past history to score points. What is important is what is happening now, what the feelings and issues are now. The past cannot be modified, the present can. (This is not to say that long witheld feelings should not be expressed. At an appropriate place and time, such a disclosure can be extremely helpful.)

Step four. Use polarization constructively. People sometimes desire or need to get away from each other in the midst of a conflict, either because anger has escalated beyond manageable limits, or just to think more clearly. Such polarization or time apart should be used constructively, to cool off or figure out how to move closer together on the issue at hand and resolve the conflict. Such time should not be used destructively, to figure out how to get even or perpetuate the conflict.

Step five. Find out what each partner has in common regarding the issue at hand. The common ground, or items both partners agree upon already, is frequently overshadowed by the differences. Identification of the common ground helps the couple to see the differences in perspective, and frequently provides a positive starting place from which to build a constructive solution.

Step six. Mutual problem-solving. The couple identifies many possible solutions to the problem, and the positive and negative consequences of each. A joint decision is reached to pursue one proposed solution, which is followed by the creation of an agreed upon action plan which includes specific steps and a time sequence. (See Contract Writing.)

Step seven. Coming together in celebration. Some signal is given, through the use of words or touch, to signify resolution of the conflict, or that they have at least agreed to disagree, or that they have gone as far as they can at this time, or that the conflict will not remain a permanent barrier in the relationship. For example, a couple could use a hug, kiss or other constructive use of physical touch, including sexual relationships; or, words could be used, such as "I love you and I'm glad we worked this out," "Thanks for hanging in there with me," or "Let's put it aside for now and come back to it later."

For the next five to ten minutes, each couple is asked to discuss areas of conflict between them, and to decide one issue they are willing to deal with openly, in a total group setting. The total group is reconvened and one volunteer couple is requested to be the focus couple for this experience. No couple is accepted unless both partners are clearly willing to participate. We emphasize that the volunteer couple may not have sufficient time to fully resolve the issue, but that we will stay with the interaction until an appropriate stopping point is reached. We stress that the purpose of the experience is to develop skills in the effective use of conflict.

In over fifty experiences, we have never failed to have a volunteer couple emerge from the group. However, before a volunteer couple is requested, we clearly emphasize that if no couple volunteers, we will use a conflict role play, which can be a very effective learning experience, using volunteer individuals, and the procedure which is described following. In this way, we hope to reduce pressure on couples to participate.

When a couple has volunteered, chairs are arranged in the following fashion: two chairs for the volunteer couple, facing each other in the center of the group; four chairs about six feet directly behind each of the first two for coaching teams, and chairs around the periphery for observers.

After the stage has been set, each partner of the volunteer couple is requested to select two couples to serve as a coaching team for the duration of the conflict resolution experience. It is explained that the role of the coaching teams will be to support each participant, help clarify what each wants to say, help to identify blocks, and offer alternative ways of interacting. As each coaching team couple is selected, they take their seats directly behind the person who selected them. Couples not selected as coaches take their seats on the periphery, and serve as observers. The volunteer couple are requested to sit facing each other in the center of the group, just to get the feel of the setting. The stage-setting and selecting of coaching teams phase of the experience takes no more than five minutes.

After a few minutes, the two partners are sent to their coaching teams for ten minutes. Each is instructed to inform the coaching team of the nature of the conflict, how he intends to pursue the issue, what the desired outcome is, and so on. The task of the coaching team is to listen empathically, help clarify the issue, challenge assumptions, help to uncover underlying feelings, and identify anticipated blocks to resolving the conflict.

Our experience has been that although a discussion, "How to Have a Good Clean Fight," has been presented just a few minutes prior, participants will utilize their normal style of coping with conflict. Hurt feelings are frequently forgotten or overlooked; the conflict is seen as win-lose, rather than as having the potential to be resolved in an "I win-you win" fashion; many people quickly push for premature problem-solving. The leadership couple observes the interaction in each of the coaching teams (one partner to each team), but makes no intervention into the process at this time.

When the ten minutes have elapsed, the volunteer couple is requested to sit facing each other in the center of the group. Each coaching team is instructed to observe the interaction, paying attention to verbal and nonverbal dimensions, what is perceived to be helpful, unhelpful, and so on. The observers are given the same instructions. We emphasize again that the conflict issue may not be fully resolved during this experience, and that our major goal is to increase conflict utilization skills. The volunteer couple is instructed to begin interaction, with the reminder that they will periodically be given the opportunity to return to the coaching team for support and help. The leadership couple monitors the interaction, but makes no intervention at this point. The couple is permitted to continue as long as the leadership couple perceives the interaction to be helpful. If and when a block emerges (usually after about ten minutes), the interaction is stopped and the partners return to their coaching teams to express their feelings and discuss what has been happening that is helpful and unhelpful. The observing group is instructed to huddle and express feelings and perceptions of what has been helpful and not helpful.

At this point, the leadership couple moves between the coaching team and the observer group, facilitating the discussion, and reminding participants to refer to the steps noted in the discussion. Efforts to push for a

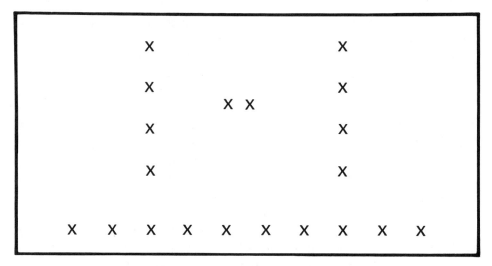

Figure 8.2. *Conflict Utilzation: Chair Arrangement*

win-lose solution are capped, and a feeling-focus is emphasized. Efforts at problem-solving are affirmed as helpful, but possibly ill-timed. The presence or absence of effective listening is discussed, since participants are frequently so wrapped up in making their own point that they fail to hear the words and sense the feelings of the other person. This second coaching phase lasts about ten minutes.

The couple then begins the conflict interaction again (usually for about twenty minutes), using the feedback from the previous coaching session. As the interaction progresses, members of the leadership couple may actively intervene to facilitate the interaction (e.g., to help clarify the feelings or issue, to encourage the couple to touch or hold hands as a hurt feeling emerges, to encourage a less verbal partner to express thoughts or feelings, to request that one partner use the skill of parroting, paraphrasing or total listening, etc.). At an appropriate point, a brief coaching session may be held. If a member of a couple is blocked in expressing his thoughts or feelings, he may be requested to select a member of the coaching team to sit with him during the interaction, to be supportive and perhaps even speak briefly for him.

By this time, most of the group is usually identifying very strongly with the volunteer couple, and a lot of feeling is usually present. We believe one of the main tasks of the coaching team is to help the volunteer couple to express feelings to each other, especially the hurt feelings and whatever fears might be present. Active intervention on the part of the leadership team will help prevent destructive escalation of angry feelings, and bring the experience to a close at an appropriate point. As the experience is being brought to a close, we sit quite close to the volunteer couple, and we encourage them, as they sit in the center of the group, to talk together briefly about what they experienced and are feeling and thinking. We encourage them to give some verbal or nonverbal expression of caring to each other, to indicate their affection for each other, and to signal resolution of the conflict or that they are willing to put it aside for the time being. We will frequently give them a hug ourselves and affirm their efforts and express our appreciation for being willing to be the focus couple. We also request that both coaching teams give the volunteer couple a group hug, with the volunteers at the center of the group. The debriefing of the couple usually takes about ten minutes.

The total group then debriefs the experience for about fifteen minutes, expressing their own feelings and discussing what they perceived to be helpful and unhelpful. The coaching teams and observers are usually quite insightful, and it quickly becomes evident that many identifications were made with the process of conflict management demonstrated by the volunteer couple. Reference is made to the discussion "How To Have A Good Clean Fight," and it is emphasized again that the conflict utilization is a skill that can be learned, practiced and used effectively.

To complete the experience, each person is offered the opportunity to say and complete the following statement: "One thing I do that is helpful in a conflict with (partner's name) is . . ." When those who want to express themselves have done so, each person is offered a second opportunity to say and complete the following statement: "One thing I do that is helpful in a conflict with (partner's name) is . . . ." The openness and depth of sharing that emerges at this point is often a moving experience. We then encourage each couple to share a hug and kiss and end with a group hug.

We have used this Conflict Utilization experience in many different settings and have found it to be a highly valued and helpful experience for participants. In a weekend setting, there is usually sufficient time for only one couple to be the focus couple. However, the identifications that take place as the conflict process unfolds allow virtually all participants to learn something from the experience. In a multi-week setting, more couples have the opportunity to be the focus couple, and there is a greater opportunity to practice effective conflict utilization skills. In an open-ended, multi-week enrichment experience, we have spent as many as six two-hour sessions on conflict utilization.

We want to emphasize that the conflict utilization exprience presented here requires a skilled and understanding leadership couple or team. Experience and training in effective utilization of conflict (using the theoretical model discussed earlier), in group process, and in facilitating the expression of hurt and angry feelings between partners and capping such feelings when appropriate, is crucial. Individuals and couples who are anxious, afraid of, and unable to manage strong expressions of such feelings should not attempt to lead this experience with married couples. Instead, a role-play model using non-spouse role-players should be considered as a helpful alternative. We cannot overstate the importance of qualified leadership for this conflict utilization experience, which closes the control section of the Creative Marriage Enrichment Program.

9

The Creative Marriage Enrichment Program: Affection

The interpersonal need for affection is defined as the need to "establish and maintain a satisfactory relationship with others with respect to love and affection. Some terms that connote aspects of primarily positive affection are love, like, emotionally close, personal, intimate, friend, sweetheart. Aspects of negative affection are connoted by hate, cool, dislike, emotionally distant, rejection" (Schutz, 1978, p. 8). The third section of the Creative Marriage Enrichment Program is designed to primarily address this interpersonal need for affection.

HAND EXPLORATION

Objectives: The objectives of the Hand Exploration experience are: to experience a wide range of feelings toward one's partner, to experience a sense of emotional intimacy with one's partner, and to share feelings of marital intimacy with another couple.

Time: Twenty-five minutes.

Procedure: This is a *nonverbal* experience. Partners are instructed to stand facing each other. They are to hold hands and breathe deeply, to relax. Couples frequently giggle with anxiety at this point, and we encourage them to laugh and get it out of their system. As the laughter subsides, we ask partners to look at each other and sense the feelings each has for the other person. They are to maintain eye contact, but not to stare.

After a few moments, the leader, using a slow pace, with time between each phrase, instructs the couples to remember certain significant events from their past. For example, "remember the first time you met each other; remember the day you agreed to marry each other; remember the day you got married; remember the first time you shared sexual intercourse; remember the first time you had a significant argument or fight; if you have children, remember the time you held your first child together for the first time; remember the moments of closeness in your relationship, the moments of distance, the times of happiness, the times of sadness."

After the significant events are highlighted, participants are asked to identify how they are feeling towards each other at that moment. They are then requested to close their eyes and stand silently together, being aware of the presence of the other person. Instructions are given to explore each other's hands, taking turns, being aware of the size, texture, temperature, and unique characteristics. After a few minutes of exploration, each couple is requested to express certain things, nonverbally, through the hand-to-hand contact. For example: "say hello; express happiness, sadness, playfulness, sensousness; have an argument and express anger; make up; show love and affection; realize that this is the last time you will ever hold those hands again; say good-bye; *let go*; feel what it is like to be without your partner; now realize you can get back together; have a reunion; celebrate your togetherness; now stand still, with your hands held between you; breathe deeply; when you are ready, open your eyes and nonverbally greet each other." This initial phase, from the time couples first stand facing each other, to the point when they open their eyes and greet each other, usually takes about ten minutes.

The second phase of the experience involves two couples talking together for ten minutes regarding what they experienced and what they felt during the hand-holding phase. The experience concludes with a five minute segment during which the total group verbalizes thoughts and feelings regarding the experience.

Couples frequently find this to be a deeply moving experience, as they remember the feelings associated with significant events from the past, moments of closeness and distance, happiness and sadness. Letting go of the other's hands is very difficult for some couples to do, and we frequently must wait a significant period of time for that to occur. Many participants report that simulating the last time they will ever hold those hands again gives them a sense of the grief they anticipate they would experience if the spouse were to die. These are feelings and thoughts which they had never experienced before or had suppressed or avoided. In many people, it also affirms how much they value and love their partner, despite the presence of little irritations or even major differences, some of which may have become evident during the Conflict Utilization experience. The Hand Exploration frequently serves as a healing experience after the experience of conflict, and contributes to an increase in pair-bonding and emotional intimacy for most couples.

MARITAL INTIMACY CHECK-UP*

Objectives: The objectives of the Marital Intimacy Check-Up experience are to gain an understanding of the many facets of intimacy (i.e., that it is more than sexual intimacy), to identify and verbalize areas of strength in intimacy and areas of needed or desired growth and development, and to plan for change in the marital relationship to deepen the experience of one or more of the various facets of intimacy.

Time: Forty-five minutes.

Procedures: A Marital Intimacy Check-Up form (Clinebell and Clinebell, 1970) and a Marital Intimacy Action Plan form (Clinebell and Clinebell, 1970) are distributed to each couple. They are instructed to read over each of the definitions of the twelve facets of intimacy described on the Marital Intimacy Check-Up form. They are to discuss each facet of intimacy with respect to their marital relationship. If both are satisfied with the level of intimacy in the area being considered they should affirm that to each other and check the appropriate space. If one or both partners desires improvement in the area being considered, that should be openly expressed and a check placed in the appropriate space. The couple then moves on to the next facet of intimacy and repeats the process until all twelve areas of intimacy have been considered and discussed.

Marital Intimacy Check-up

1) Check the blanks that apply to your relationship.
2) Discuss each area.
3) Share your feelings.

THE MANY FACETS OF INTIMACY

	Both desire improve- ment	Wife desires improve- ment	Husband desires improve- ment	Both satisfied
Sexual Intimacy Sensual–emotional satisfaction; the experience of sharing and self-abandon in the merging of two persons; experimental, growing, expanding, and honest openness; fantasies and desires; totally becoming one flesh, freedom, joy, fun, etc.	_____	_____	_____	_____

*If time limitations necessitate the removal of one or more experiences from the program, the Marital Intimacy Check-Up and the Love-Life Development Test which follows could be possible options. Either or both of these experiences can be explained briefly and given as homework tasks to be accomplished after the weekend is over. Such an approach would also give couples an opportunity to continue the enrichment experience in their back-home environment.

	Both desire improve-ment	Wife desires improve-ment	Husband desires improve-ment	Both satisfied

Emotional Intimacy

Being tuned to each other's wavelength; the foundation of all other forms and facets of intimacy; depth awareness and sharing of significant meanings and feelings; the touching of the innermost selves of two human beings; closeness, warmth, desire, etc.

Intellectual Intimacy

Closeness in the world of ideas; sharing the world of ideas; a genuine touching of persons based on mutual respect for each other's intellectual capacities; sharing mind-stretching and expanding experiences; reading–discussing–studying, etc.

Aesthetic Intimacy

Sharing experiences of beauty—music, nature, art, theater, dance, movies; drinking from the common cup of beauty wherever it is found, etc.

Creative Intimacy

Sharing in acts of creating together; helping each other to grow, to be co-creators (not reformers) of each other; mutually feeding each other so that each can realize his potentialities as a person; seeing marriage relationship as a joint venture into a life of growth, etc.

Recreational Intimacy

Relating in experiences of fun and play; sharing ways of refilling the wells of energy; allowing the Child in each other to rejuvenate the personality through stress-relieving and fun play, etc.

Work Intimacy

The closeness of sharing common tasks, such as maintaining a house and yard, raising a family, earning a living, and participating in community affairs and concerns; joining strengths and supporting each other in bearing responsibilities, etc.

	Both desire improve- ment	Wife desires improve- ment	Husband desires improve- ment	Both satisfied
Crisis Intimacy Closeness in coping with problems and pain; standing together against the buffeting of fate; standing together in the major and minor trag- edies which persist in life; internal testing, pres- sures of aging, struggling with differences, con- flict utilization, etc.	————	————	————	————
Commitment Intimacy The sense of togetherness derived from com- mon self-investment; shared dedication; trust; turned on by a common cause or value, etc.	————	————	————	————
Spiritual Intimacy The "we-ness" of sharing ultimate concerns; shar- ing the meanings of life, discovering and shar- ing a foundation ground, center, core; sharing a firm foundation or supportive ground for tran- sient human relatedness; values; worthfulness; religion, etc.	————	————	————	————
Communication Intimacy Keeping channels open; being honest, trusting, truthful, loving; giving feedback; confrontation, etc.	————	————	————	————
Conflict Intimacy Facing and struggling with differences together, etc.	————	————	————	————

Marital Intimacy Action Plan

(To follow Marital Intimacy Check-Up)

Note the following points:

In those areas in which you both desire improvement, discuss specific next steps which you feel can be taken to increase the degree of mutuality and meaningful closeness in each area.

If you agree on specific action in one or more areas, decide on how you will go about implementing your plan.

If you agree on what you want to do in several areas, decide on which should have priority.

Jot down the main ideas for action under the appropriate categories below:

Sexual Intimacy:
Emotional Intimacy:
Intellectual Intimacy:
Aesthetic Intimacy:
Creative Intimacy:
Recreational Intimacy:
Work Intimacy:
Crisis Intimacy:
Conflict Intimacy:
Commitment Intimacy:
Spiritual Intimacy:
Communication Intimacy:
Notes:

Couples are reminded that time considerations preclude the possibility of creating an appropriate Marital Intimacy Action Plan or Contract for each of the areas in which one or both partners desire improvement. However, they are encouraged to begin the process of planning for change by focusing on at least one area in which both desire improvement or change. We encourage them to complete the process after the weekend is over, and to continue to make plans aimed at increasing intimacy between them.

Using the Marital Intimacy Action Plan, each couple is to discuss specific steps they believe can be taken which will result in increased satisfaction and intimacy in the area under consideration. When agreement is reached on a specific action, it should be noted on the Marital Intimacy Action Plan. The couple may simply agree to follow through on the action plan when they return home or they may write a contract, using the guidelines established earlier. If, within the time available, a couple is able to decide on an action plan in more than one area of intimacy, they are to decide which should have priority. During the final five minutes of the experience, each couple is requested to verbalize feelings which were experienced during the Marital Intimacy Check-Up and the creation of the Marital Intimacy Action Plan.

LOVE-LIFE DEVELOPMENT TEST

Objectives: The objectives of the Love-Life Development Test experience are to develop or increase the ability to openly discuss the sexual relationship in marriage, and to identify and express areas of strength in sexual expression in the marital relationship, as well as areas of needed or desired growth and development.

Time: Fifty minutes.

Procedure: The leadership couple begins this experience by giving some brief input (about ten minutes) regarding the difficulty that many couples have openly discussing their sexual desires, needs, and expectations of each other. In addition, they note the great lack of knowledge that many couples still have with respect to sexuality, despite the proliferation of many books and articles on the subject. The importance of clear and direct communication in the sexual area, as well as all other areas of the marital relationship, is stressed. The sharing of examples or vignettes from their own lives will personalize the input and increase the ability of the participants to identify with it.

A Love-Life Development Test (Otto, 1969) is distributed to each participant, and the instructions are explained (about five minutes). It is emphasized that the purpose of the test is to increase communication between partners regarding their sexual relationship, and to identify and affirm areas of satisfaction and strength as well as areas of needed or desired growth and development. It is also stressed that due to differences in individual interpretations and preferences, the answers any two partners give will never exactly coincide. Such differences are affirmed as natural and healthy. What is sought is deeper understanding, not agreement on some markings on a piece of paper.

*Love-Life Development Test**

Frank communication between husbands and wives about their love life can lead to a more satisfying marital relationship. The purpose of the Love-Life Development Test is to help you in the continuing development of a more satisfying love life.

The Love-Life Development Test is divided into three sections, entitled *Love Play, Intercourse,* and *After Intercourse.* Do not score your test until you have finished marking all the items. Scoring instructions will be found at the end of the test.

After you have completed filling out your copy of the test, husband and wife can place their copies of the Love-Life Development Test side by side and compare their markings. It is of the utmost importance to recognize that due to individual differences the markings will never exactly coincide and that differences are normal and natural.

The greatest values and benefits from this test arise from the frank communication and exchange between husband and wife as they discuss their test results together. The more open and free the communication is the greater the possibility for positive gains in the relationship.

Now read each item in the test. Ask yourself the following question: "In relation to each item, how much do we need to develop our love life?"

Then, on the development scale, circle whether you need much development, some development, little development (which means things are pretty good) or none (which means everything is fine).

---

*This test was developed by Herbert A. Otto in *More Joy in Your Marriage,* 1969. It is included here, in modified form and with expanded definitions, by permission of the author.

Section I: Love Play

1. Giving each other tenderness and affection in everyday living (not as an approach to, or way of asking for, intercourse).
   Development needed: Much   Some   Little   None

2. Giving each other enough understanding and consideration daily and not only as a means of leading up to intercourse.
   Development needed: Much   Some   Little   None

3. Creating a romantic atmosphere by, for example, having a candlelight dinner, bringing flowers or other surprises.
   Development needed: Much   Some   Little   None

4. Bathing, perfuming or anointing the body.
   Development needed: Much   Some   Little   None

4a. Too much bathing, perfuming or anointing the body. (Underline which; strike out if not applicable. Note: No point score for this item.)
   Development needed: Much   Some   Little   None

5. Having sufficient privacy together.
   Development needed: Much   Some   Little   None

6. Loving stimulation of sensitive body areas.
   Development needed: Much   Some   Little   None

7. Gentle and loving caressing and manipulation of sex organs.
   Development needed: Much   Some   Little   None

8. Strong and concentrated caressing and manipulating of sex organs.
   Development needed: Much   Some   Little   None

9. New ideas for love play. (Suggest some.)
   Development needed: Much   Some   Little   None

10. Reading articles or books or discussing together ways to enhance and enrich love play, or sharing fantasies (underline which).
   Development needed: Much   Some   Little   None

11. Setting the atmosphere for love play and intercourse by: Relaxing together with a drink (cordial, wine, etc.) or other treat. Using light caresses to engender loving feelings. Using a stimulating fragrance (scented candles, incense, etc.).
   Other:
   Development needed: Much   Some   Little   None

12. Experimenting with love play and intercourse at unusual hours, such as middle of the night (mid-sleep), early morning, after cocktails and before dinner, outdoors in a sunny retreat, etc.
   Development needed: Much   Some   Little   None

13. Plan a second honeymoon weekend (or night) together away from the family, or (suggest others).
   Development needed: Much   Some   Little   None

Total Point Score for Love Play Section:

Section II: Intercourse

1. Sensitivity to each other's moods and feelings during intercourse.
   Development needed: Much   Some   Little   None

2. More prolonged intercourse.
   Development needed: Much   Some   Little   None

3. *More* or *Less* (circle which) body movement during intercourse.
   Development needed: Much   Some   Little   None

4. Achieving a satisfactory climax.
   Development needed: Much   Some   Little   None

5. Frequency or number of times of intercourse.
   Development needed: Much   Some   Little   None

5a. Desired frequency weekly: . (Note: No point score for this item).
   Development needed: Much   Some   Little   None

6. Having orgasm by other means, such as: a. Mouth-genital; b. Hands-genital; c. Mouth-breasts-hands-genital; d. Other
   Development needed: Much   Some   Little   None

7. Investigating other contraceptive methods.
   Development needed: Much   Some   Little   None

8. Using different positions in intercourse.
   Development needed: Much   Some   Little   None

9. Exploring and thinking through (by discussing) the role of spiritual elements in intercourse and sexual expression.
   Development needed: Much   Some   Little   None

10. Reading a book together on different techniques of intercourse.
    Development needed: Much   Some   Little   None

11. New ideas for intercourse. (Suggest some.)
    Development needed: Much   Some   Little   None

12. Exploring and thinking through (by discussing) the role of different emotional elements in intercourse and sexual expression.
    Development needed: Much   Some   Little   None

Total Point Score for Intercourse Section:

Section III: After Intercourse

1. Expressing love, tenderness and affection after intercourse.
   Development needed: Much   Some   Little   None

2. Length of time spent together after intercourse.
   Development needed: Much   Some   Little   None

3. Doing something for the partner after intercourse, such as serving a snack or (suggest some).
   Development needed: Much   Some   Little   None

4. Repeated intercourse following the first time.
   Development needed: Much   Some   Little   None

5. Creating a different pattern—doing something different after intercourse.
   Development needed: Much   Some   Little   None

        Total Point Score for After Intercourse Section:

Scoring Instructions

Score each section only after you have completed filling out the entire test.
        Add the point score for each item and fill in the total score at the end of each section.
        To arrive at a total score for each section, add together the point score for each item, using scoring table provided.
        Now take your total score from each section and enter it on the profile by marking an X to the left of the corresponding number of the Point Score Index of the Love-Life Development Profile.
        After you have entered your scores from all three sections on the Love-Life Development Profile, connect the X's on the profile. This gives you a visual index or map of the developmental aspects of your love life.

The Meaning of Your Profile and Point Score

The more your map falls in the area entitled "development needed" the greater the likelihood that, in order to achieve increased satisfaction, you need to work on the particular area, such as Love Play, Intercourse, or After Intercourse *together*.
        Remember: The greatest values and benefits from this test arise from the frank communication and exchange between husband and wife as they go over their tests together.
        Husband and wife can place their Love-Life Development Profile side by side and compare scores. It is of the utmost importance to recognize, however, that due to individual differences the point scores will never exactly coincide and that differences are natural and normal.
        You may also wish to review your marking of each section together by placing the tests side by side and talking over the various items as you go along. The greater your frankness and freedom in discussion, the greater the possibility of direct and immediate benefits.
        In the event that great differences have been uncovered as a result of using this test, it may be well to consult a marriage counselor as another means of improving your relationship.

        Each individual is given fifteen minutes to complete the form, circling the word "much," "some," "little," or "none," whichever indicates the amount of development needed in that particular area of the sexual relationship. For example, in Section I: Love Play, item one, if the wife believes that little development is needed in "giving each other tenderness and affection in everyday living (not as an approach to, or way of asking for, intercourse)," she will circle the word, "Little."

        When each person has completed the form, partners meet to discuss their respective answers (about twenty minutes). Some people find it

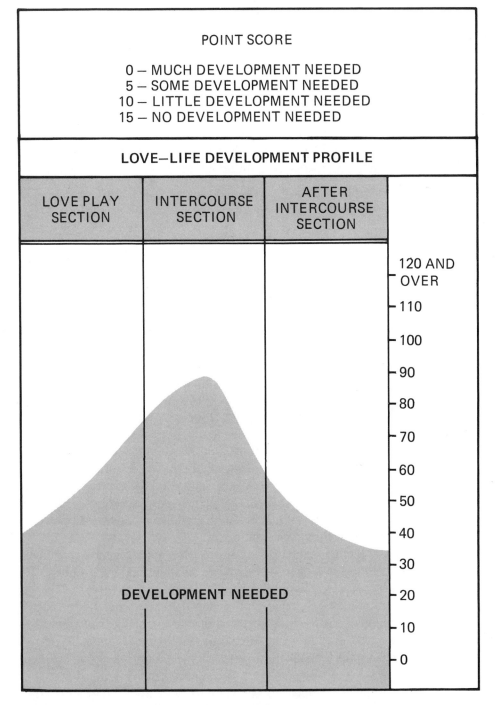

Figure 9.1. *Love-Life Development Test: Point Score and Profile*

helpful to place their tests side by side to compare answers. Frank and open discussion is encouraged, along with empathic listening. We suggest that couples clearly affirm those areas in which they are both satisfied and note those areas in which development is needed or desired. We suggest that they clearly express their desires and expectations to each other, but postpone the making of a definitive Marital Intimacy Action Plan or Contract until they return home from the weekend. They will then be able to devote a sufficient amount of time to the accomplishment of that task. In addition, the delay in completing this phase of the Love-Life Development Test serves the purpose of encouraging the participants to continue the enrichment process when the weekend is over.

PLEASURING

Objectives: The objectives of the Pleasuring experience are to express and receive feelings of intimacy in a nonverbal, physical fashion, and to increase bonding in the relationship through the sharing of unconditional positive regard.

Time: Twenty-five minutes.

Procedure: Pleasuring is defined as the giving and receiving of physical touch that is perceived as satisfying and enjoyable by both the giver and the receiver. It is emphasized, for example, that a husband gives of himself by not only pleasuring his wife, but also by receiving, by permitting his wife to give of herself by pleasuring him. Of course, the same principle applies for either partner. Pleasuring is thus a gift of the self in the giving and the receiving. It is noted that pleasuring can be in the form of a gentle back-rub, a facial massage, a foot or hand massage, or a full body massage. Though tired, tense or aching muscles are frequently relieved through the experience, the emphasis is upon giving and receiving pleasure and sharing intimacy rather than upon relief of muscular aches, pains or tensions. It should take place in a relaxed, unhurried atmosphere.

Couples are given the opportunity to experience a gentle facial massage. Paper towels and small cups containing a small amount of a water-based lotion are distributed to each couple. The leadership couple emphasizes the nonverbal nature of the experience, and models the experience for the participants. The giving of instructions and demonstration of the massage takes about five minutes. Couples are instructed to take twenty minutes to do the pleasuring, ten minutes for each partner.

Partners are instructed to put some space between themselves and other couples, to avoid distractions. They are to sit facing each other, or one can lie with his head in the other's lap, whichever feels more comfortable. They are to look at each other in silence for a few moments, and to sense their feelings of warmth for each other. The giver then proceeds to gently massage the face of the receiver, tracing the lines of the face, as a sculptor might, and gently caressing and massaging the forehead, jaw, cheeks, temples, and so on. The use of a small amount of hand lotion (properly warmed by rubbing into the giver's hands before application to the face of the receiver), reduces friction and it may be used or not in addition to the gentle massage. When the giver has completed the massage, he is to communicate that with some nonverbal expression, such as a kiss or a light touch on the arm. The receiver is to lie silently for a few moments. Partners then reverse roles and repeat the process.

SERVICE OF COMMITMENT

Objectives: The objectives of the Service of Commitment experience are to increase and affirm the sense of commitment to each other, to request, and give forgiveness for perceived wrongs in the relationship, and to place the marital relationship within the framework of the couple's spiritual life and value system.

Time: Thirty-five minutes.

Procedure: Three Service of Commitment handouts* are available for use. We have two of them available for participant couples to select from when the group is mixed according to religious orientation. One is classified Non-Religious Focus, the other Religious Focus. The only difference between the two is the presence of a prayer in the latter and some direct references to God. The differences are only present in the section that each couple does in private. The total group sections of the experience are identical. When we work with groups with a Christian orientation, the Christian Focus handout is used, containing direct references to Jesus Christ and the experience of Holy Communion. Of course, the Communion experience is used only when an appropriately trained and ordained clergyperson is part of the leadership team.

In all three variations, a paraphrase of Paul's writing about love, from I Corinthians 13 in the New Testament of the Bible, is used. Since the Bible is part of the literature of the world, we do not believe the inclusion of a paraphrased portion of it in any way contributes to making the experience more religious for non-religiously oriented participants than would the inclusion of any other piece of literature. However, for some such participants, the renewal of marriage vows (done in privacy) does have direct religious impli-

---

*Because of the length and similarity of the three Service of Commitment handouts, they appear as Appendix C at the back of the book.

cations. For those couples who find this objectionable, we urge that they do not participate in that part of the experience, and use that time in a way that would be more meaningful for them. In fact, with all three variations, we encourage couples to modify the section done in privacy according to their own needs (e.g., they may not like the vows we have written, and would prefer to verbalize their own). We do, however, encourage them not to omit something just because it might be uncomfortable (e.g., Experience of Forgiveness).

The vast majority of participants use the Service of Commitment as written, and many report it to be a significant and intimate experience. Each one of the three forms contains all of the instructions for each of the couples to follow as they go off for fifteen minutes by themselves. However, we generally take about five minutes to give an overview of the experience. The forms also include the instructions for the Total Group section (fifteen minutes) which immediately follows the portion each couple completes alone.

The Experience of Forgiveness has been reported by many couples to be helpful in managing guilt for perceived wrongs experienced in the relationship. We are continually surprised by the number of people who have never requested forgiveness from their partner or verbally affirmed forgiveness to their partner. For many, it is a liberating and intimate experience.

The renewing of marriage vows is designed to deepen the sense of personal commitment to the marital relationship. The voluntary Statement of Affirmation is designed to give individuals the opportunity to openly and verbally affirm their marital relationship. The experience ends with a group hug, during which participants are encouraged to make eye contact with each other and to be aware of their feelings towards each other. The group then drops arms and participates in the Evaluation and Closure experience.

The Service of Commitment experience is frequently a high emotional experience for some participants. We do not like to end the program on such an emotional high, and therefore choose to immediately follow it with the Evaluation and Closure experience. We believe this facilitates re-entry to the back home situation by diminishing the gap between the emotionally high situation and the realities of the everyday life to which participants will soon be returning, with household chores, children, and work. For this reason, we follow the Evaluation and Closure experience with an evening meal. This permits couples to slowly withdraw from the experience and from relationships which have been brief but intense. We believe this contributes to the reduction of the emotional shock participants can experience if careful attention is not paid to re-entry issues. That shock cannot be completely avoided, but if couples are informed that it might occur, and if the end of the program is designed in such a way as to minimize it, its impact may be significantly diminished.

EVALUATION AND CLOSURE

Objectives: The objectives of the Evaluation and Closure experience are to identify and express learnings and feelings from the marriage enrichment program and to bring a sense of closure to the program.

Time: Forty-five minutes.

Procedure: An evaluation sheet is distributed to each participant. It contains six incomplete statements.

Evaluation Sheet

Please complete the following:

1. I learned . . .
2. I liked . . .
3. I felt most comfortable . . .
4. I felt most uncomfortable . . .
5. I was disappointed . . .
6. I wish we had . . .

When you have completed this form meet with your partner and one other couple and share as much or as little of what you have written as you want to.

Each individual is instructed to take about ten minutes to complete the six statements. When everybody has completed the form, two couples meet together and share with each other as much or as little of what they have written as each person desires. This small group process usually takes about twenty minutes. It is followed by the total group being reconvened, with everyone being given the opportunity to verbalize general or specific evaluative comments to the leadership couple (about ten minutes).

The experience concludes with the formation of a group circle with participants standing with arms around each other. They are once more requested to survey the group and make eye contact with as many people as possible, being aware of their feelings for those persons. Physical contact is broken and participants are encouraged to say their individual good-byes. (With some groups, closing the final group circle with a statement such as, "Now let's go and experience life with our families and friends as husbands and wives living together in love," may be appropriate). The group is reminded that the weekend program ends with the evening meal.

Epilogue

I gladly accept the invitation of the authors to contribute an epilogue to this book.

I do so because, in my judgment, what it presents is accurate, sound, and convincing. No other publication has, to my knowledge, put together as yet such a felicitous combination of material concerning the new and very promising field of marriage enrichment. Beginning with a broad and well-balanced survey of the entire field, it then describes, in great detail, an actual marriage enrichment program which in my opinion must be ranked with the best that have so far been developed.

The book therefore provides the reader with a clear and full picture. If you have read it with attention, you now know most of what anyone at present knows about the subject. And I would further add that this is a subject in which, in my opinion, a great number of people are going to want to be well informed during the next ten years. Let me try to explain why I take that view.

Human society is, in a sense that has never been so true in time past, at a point of crisis. Vast cultural changes have, in our life-time, opened up prospects which engender in us, as we look to the future, both dazzling hopes and numbing fears. Science and technology have opened up revolutionary possibilities that boggle the mind. We are in fact no longer talking about "the future," but about "futures"—a vast array of options which now confront us. Of the many directions in which we can now go, which shall we take? The making of that choice wisely could lead us to the fulfillment of man's most ambitious hopes. Unwisely made, the choice could lead to stark disaster.

Can we act wisely? Yes, surely, if we go forward together hand in hand, achieving our human destiny in harmonious cooperation, mutually trusting and supporting each other. In order to do this, however, we must achieve one goal above all others—we must improve the quality of our relationships.

In this century we have harnessed the power of the atom and probed the inner secrets of the cell. We have penetrated outer space. We have made giant strides toward the conquest of disease. We have seen the possibility of improving living standards beyond the wildest dreams of our forefathers.

Yet with all these achievements, we have so far failed dismally to improve the quality of human relationships. Hate, suspicion, and greed are with us as they have always been—and their destructive power has been exponentially increased.

Now the last frontier confronts us. Unless we can find a way for human beings to live together in peace and harmony, all the glittering prizes we have won may be lost.

My professional life began in a London slum in the 1930s, in the depths of the Depression. I saw widespread suffering and misery and was compelled to look for answers. A few years later I witnessed the horrors of war as the bombs rained down and helpless, innocent people were murdered and mutilated through "man's inhumanity to man." Still I was looking for answers. Amid all the destruction and hate I kept meeting beautiful people who loved and cared. But there were not enough of them to take over and fashion a society that would be based on mutual cooperation and integrity.

How can we greatly increase the number of caring and loving people? That was, and still is, the critical question.

For myself, I found the answer. I saw clearly that human families were the factories where people are made—or marred. As a counselor, I saw how people were twisted and hardened, early in life, when they lived in loveless homes—loveless because men and women who sought joy and intimacy and tenderness in marriage failed to find what they sought, for all their earnest striving. I tried to help such people by establishing counseling services. I opened the first continuing marriage counseling agency in Europe, and saw it grow and multiply. As the years passed, I saw knowledge increase as the behavioral sciences, though still far behind the physical and biological sciences, gradually developed and came of age. I began to cherish the hope that at long last we might focus our attention on the most vital goal of all—the understanding of close, intimate relationships, and the discovery of how to nourish and support such relationships so that they could produce loving, caring people—the kind of people we need so desperately.

Progress has been slow, but we are getting nearer and nearer to our goal. We are finally beginning to learn the art of teaching men and women to achieve *their* goals—not goals we want to impose upon them, but goals they deeply and earnestly long for and strive for themselves. If only we can make that possible, and then multiply the process on an ever-increasing scale, a vast transformation of human relationships could result in time, and we would release a positive power that could be more revolutionary than any previous revolution in human history.

Too long have we clung to the illusion that the basic unit of human society is the individual. An individual does not develop identity in isolation. Our children begin life with an inheritance of undeveloped and undifferentiated potential—for good or for evil—and they become persons through continuous interaction with other individuals with whom they meet and mingle. The true unit of human society is therefore the *dyad*—two individuals, interacting with each other, and in the process, making and molding each other's identity.

. I see this book as a harbinger of new beginnings. It tells the story of how at last we are digging down to the very roots of human society—close dyadic relationships—and helping them to become, by the flowering of the rich potential for love that is within them, the best that they are capable of becoming.

The cynics may dismiss all this as starry-eyed idealism, just as they did long ago when men of faith looked out over the desert and glimpsed the shimmering outlines of the Promised Land. I am content to say to the unbelieving, "Ten years from now, I predict that marriage and family enrichment will have developed resources that will make possible, for the many, relationships of a quality now experienced only by the few. And when that time comes, it may indeed be possible, on such a broad-based foundation, to begin the task of building a better and a happier world."

Dr. David Mace
Director of Marriage Enrichment and Training,
Department of Human Enrichment and Development,
North Carolina Baptist Hospitals, Inc.,
Winston-Salem, North Carolina.

Appendix A

Creative Marriage Enrichment Program

SUGGESTED SCHEDULE FOR A WEEKEND PROGRAM

Friday Evening

6:45	Arrival, Check-In, and Coffee Time
7:30	Introduction
7:40	Goal-Setting
8:15	Communication Skills
9.05	Group Circle
9:15	Free Time

Saturday Morning

9:00	Wake-Up Exercises
9:15	Marriage Life Line
9:50	Life-Time Drawing
10:45	Coffee Break
10:55	Body Shop
11:05	Discussion: Circle of Trust
11:15	My World of Feelings

Saturday Afternoon

12:30	Lunch
1:45	Wants, Needs and Fears Listing
2:35	Discussions: How People Change; Contracting
2:55	Contract Writing
3:30	Free Time for recreation, napping, reading, etc.
5:30	Dinner

Saturday Evening

7:30	Individual and Marriage Strengths Listing
9:10	Discussion: Inclusion, Control and Affection
9:35	Group Circle and Hug
9:40	Free Time

Sunday Morning

8:45	Wake-Up Exercise
9:00	"Where Are You?"
9:20	Marital Role Expectations
10:35	Coffee Break
10:45	Total Group Circle Massage
10:50	Conflict Utilization

Sunday Afternoon

12:30	Lunch
1:45	Hand Exploration
2:10	Marital Intimacy Check-Up
2:55	Break
3:05	Love-Life Development Test
3:55	Pleasuring
4:20	Service of Commitment
4:55	Evaluation and Closure
5:40	Free Time
6:00	Dinner (program ends with dinner)

Appendix B

The Creative Marriage Enrichment Program

SUGGESTED SUPPLIES FOR A WEEKEND PROGRAM

Name tags
Magic markers
Newsprint
Masking tape
Spiral notebook for each participant
Pencil for each participant
Legal-size (or longer) paper for Marriage Life Line experience
Crayons
Hand lotion
Small cups
Paper towels
Copy of *The Prophet*, by Kahlil Gibran
Handouts for each participant:
    My World of Feelings
    Outline of Marital Strengths
    Marital Role Expectations Sheets
    Role Renegotiation
    How To Have a Good Clean Fight
    Marital Intimacy Check-Up
    Marital Intimacy Action Plan
    Love-Life Development Test
    Service of Commitment
    Evaluation Sheet

       In addition to the handouts, which are used during the program, we provide several other handouts for participant couples to refer to at home after the experience is completed: definitions of Parroting, Paraphrasing and Total Listening, the Circle of Trust discussion, and the How People Change, and Contracting discussions.

Appendix C

Service of Commitment Handouts for the Creative Marriage Enrichment Program

NON-RELIGIOUS FOCUS

Sit facing each other, and read the following paragraph in silence:

> Our marriage is not a finished product. It is an experience, a relationship that is being created and recreated continually. It is an ongoing process to which we must commit ourselves each day, making again the decision to share life together. This marriage enrichment experience, and the vows we are about to share together, will serve as a reminder to us that in the midst of all of the possibilities of separation which are open to us we have decided again to be faithful to the commitment which we have made to each other.

Please sit in silence for a few moments, holding each other's hands, and looking at each other. Be aware of your feelings towards yourself and your feelings for your partner. Then read, in silence, the description of the Experience of Forgiveness, and when each of you has completed the reading, one of you can begin the process of sharing.

> If our marriage is to be as strong as it can be, and as deep as we would like it to be, each of us must learn and practice forgiveness. Each of us needs to actively seek forgiveness for the times when we have wronged or hurt the other, either by words or acts of omission or commission. And each of us must be willing to actively give the forgiveness that is sought. When each of us seeks forgiveness and each of us gives forgiveness, the circle is complete, and our relationship and our love for each other is deepened.

One partner, holding the other's hands, and maintaining eye contact as much as possible, says: "One thing I would like to ask your forgiveness for is . . . .", and completes the statement.

The other person hears the statement and responds, "I forgive you, because I love you."

Repeat the process with the other person requesting forgiveness. Do more than one round if you desire.

Talk together for a few moments regarding how it feels to request forgiveness from the other, and how it feels to verbally give forgiveness to each other.

An appropriate physical expression of your caring for each other completes the Experience of Forgiveness.

After your expression of caring for each other, one of you may begin the process of renewing your marriage vows by reading the appropriate vow listed below. As much as possible, please maintain physical and eye contact with each other. When one has finished, the other will begin.

For the husband: I (name) , take you,   (name) , for my wife and my friend, to hold you and be held by you, to value you and be valued by you. With you I will share my joy and my sorrow, my affirmation and my fears, my successes and my failures. I commit myself to the continued growth of our relationship, and I celebrate the joys of our togetherness and love.

For the wife: I (name) , take you   (name) , for my husband and my friend, to hold you and be held by you, to value you and be valued by you. With you I will share my joy and my sorrow, my affirmation and my fears, my successes and my failures. I commit myself to the continued growth of our relationship, and I celebrate the joys of our togetherness and love.

Then share together a kiss, or some other nonverbal expression of your love and affection for each other.

When you have completed this part of the Service of Commitment, please return to the total group and sit quietly until the other couples have returned.

In the total group, the leader will read the following paraphrase of Paul's words on love from the New Testament, with the hope that these words will reflect and represent what we give to each other and share with each other:

I will give to you a love that is patient, a love that is kind, a love that endures. I will pledge to you a love that is not jealous or possessive, a love that is not proud or selfish, a love that is not rude or inconsiderate. My love for you will not insist on its own way, will not be irritable or resentful, will not keep account of wrongs or failures. It will rejoice when good prevails. Our love will know no limit to its endurance, no end to its trust, no fading of its hope. It will outlast everything. Our love will stand when all else around us has fallen. Our love together will have three qualities: faith . . . hope . . . love, but the greatest of these will be our love for each other."

Each individual will then have the opportunity to verbally complete the following Statement of Affirmation:

"One thing I'd like to affirm about my relationship with (partner's name) is . . . ."

Participation is purely voluntary, and some couples or individuals may choose not to express themselves in this way, at this time.

When those who want to make their Statement of Affirmation have done so, the leader will read "On Love" and "On Marriage" from Kahlil Gibran's *The Prophet.*

The total group will then rise and form a circle and share a group hug, making eye contact with each other and being aware of their feelings toward each other. The group will then break and participate in the Evaluation and Closure experience.

RELIGIOUS FOCUS

Sit facing each other, and read the following paragraph in silence:

> Our marriage is not a finished product. It is an experience, a relationship that is being created and recreated continually. It is an ongoing process to which we must commit ourselves each day, making again the decision to share life together. This marriage enrichment experience, and the vows we are about to share together, will serve as a reminder to us that in the midst of all of the possibilities of separation which are open to us we have decided again to be faithful to the commitment which we have made to each other in the presence of God.

Please sit in silence for a few moments, holding each other's hands, and looking at each other. Be aware of your feelings towards yourself and your feelings for your partner. Then read, in silence, the description of the Experience of Forgiveness, and when each of you has completed the reading, one of you can begin the process of sharing.

> If our marriage is to be as strong as it can be, and as deep as we would like it to be, each of us must learn and practice forgiveness. Each of us needs to actively seek forgiveness for the times when we have wronged or hurt the other, either by words or acts of omission or commission. And each of us must be willing to actively give the forgiveness that is sought. When each of us seeks forgiveness and each of us gives forgiveness, the circle is complete, and our relationship and our love for each other is deepened.

One partner, holding the other's hands, and maintaining eye contact as much as possible, says: "One thing I would like to ask your forgiveness for is . . . ", and completes the statement.

The other person hears the statement and responds, "I forgive you, because I love you."

Repeat the process with the other person requesting forgiveness. Do more than one round if you desire.

Talk together for a few moments regarding how it feels to request forgiveness from the other, and how it feels to verbally give forgiveness to each other.

An appropriate physical expression of your caring for each other completes the Experience of Forgiveness.

After your expression of caring for each other, one of you may begin the process of renewing your marriage vows by reading the appropriate vow listed below. As much as possible, please maintain physical and eye contact with each other. When one has finished, the other will begin.

> For the husband: I   (name)   , take you,   (name)   , for my wife and my friend, to hold you and be held by you, to value you and be valued by you. With you I will share my joy and my sorrow, my affirmation and my fears, my successes and my failures. I commit myself to the continued growth of our relationship and I celebrate the joys of our togetherness and love.

> For the wife: I   (name)   , take you   (name)   , for my husband and my friend, to hold you and be held by you, to value you and be valued by you. With you I will share my joy and my sorrow, my affirmation and my fears, my successes and my failures. I commit myself to the continued growth of our relationship, and I celebrate the joys of our togetherness and love.

Then share together a kiss, or some other nonverbal expression of your love and affection for each other.

After that, pray aloud and together the following prayer:

> God, we know and experience you as love, and in your love we pray that you will affirm and bless our marriage. Help us to develop the openness and honesty, the strength and sharing, the love and vulnerability that will enable us to continue to build a beautiful relationship together. In you, in each other, and in ourselves may we grow a trusting confidence and faith that will enable us to deal with whatever the future brings. Help us to love, honor and respect each other, and to be the best of friends. May we live so close to each other and to you, and be so responsive to each other's wants and needs, that our life together will be characterized by real peace and love, by deep care and happiness, by joy and fulfillment, and by struggling creatively with our anger and our conflicts and differences. In the growth and development of the coming years, may the commitments of today remain a source of continuing and deepening joy and affection for us. Amen.

When you have completed this part of the Service of Commitment, please return to the total group and sit quietly until the other couples have returned.

In the total group, the leader will read the following paraphrase of Paul's words on love from the New Testament, with the hope that these words will reflect and represent what we give to each other and share with each other:

> I will give to you a love that is patient, a love that is kind, a love that endures. I will pledge to you a love that is not jealous or possessive, a love that is not proud or selfish, a love that is not rude or inconsiderate. My love for you will not insist on its own way, will not be irritable or resentful, will not keep account of wrongs or failures. It will rejoice when good prevails. Our love will know no limit to its endurance, no end to its trust, no fading of its hope. It will outlast everything. Our love will stand when all else around us has fallen. Our life together will have three great qualities: faith . . . hope . . . love, but the greatest of these will be our love for each other.

Each individual will then have the opportunity to verbally complete the following Statement of Affirmation:

> "One thing I'd like to affirm about my relationship with (*partner's name*) is . . . ."

Participation is purely voluntary, and some couples or individuals may choose not to express themselves in this way, at this time.

When those who want to make their Statement of Affirmation have done so, the leader will read "On Love" and "On Marriage" from Kahlil Gabran's *The Prophet*.

The total group will then rise and form a circle and share a group hug, making eye contact with each other and being aware of their feelings toward each other. The group will then break and participate in the Evaluation and Closure experience.

CHRISTIAN FOCUS

Sit facing each other, and read the following paragraph in silence:

> Our marriage is not a finished product. It is an experience, a relationship that is being created and recreated continually. It is an ongoing process to which we must commit ourselves each day, making again the decision to share life together. This marriage enrichment experience, and the vows we are about to share together, will serve as a reminder to us that in the midst of all of the possibilities of separation which are open to us we have decided again to be faithful to the commitment which we have made to each other in the presence of God.

Please sit in silence for a few moments, holding each other's hands, and looking at each other. Be aware of your feelings towards yourself and your feelings for your partner. Then read, in silence, the description of the Experience of Forgiveness, and when each of you has completed the reading, one of you can begin the process of sharing.

> If our marriage is to be as strong as it can be, and as deep as we would like it to be, each of us must learn and practice forgiveness. Each of us needs to actively seek forgiveness for the times when we have wronged or hurt the other, either by words or acts of omission or commission. And each of us must be willing to actively give the forgiveness that is sought. When each of us seeks forgiveness and each of us gives forgiveness, the circle is complete, and our relationship and our love for each other is deepened.

One partner, holding the other's hands, and maintaining eye contact as much as possible, says: "One thing I would like to ask your forgiveness for is . . . ", and completes the statement.

The other person hears the statement and responds, "I forgive you, because I love you."

Repeat the process with the other person requesting forgiveness. Do more than one round if you desire.

Talk together for a few moments regarding how it feels to request forgiveness from the other, and how it feels to verbally give forgiveness to each other.

An appropriate physical expression of your caring for each other completes the Sacrament of Forgiveness.

After your expression of caring for each other, one of you may begin the process of renewing your marriage vows by reading the appropriate vow listed below. As much as possible, please maintain physical and eye contact with each other. When one has finished, the other will begin.

> For the husband: I   (name)   , take you   (name)   , for my wife and my friend, to hold you and be held by you, to value you and be valued by you. With you I will share my joy and my sorrow, my affirmation and my fears, my successes and my failures. I commit myself to the continued growth of our relationship, and I celebrate the joys of our togetherness and love.

> For the wife: I   (name)   , take you,   (name)   , for my husband and my friend, to hold you and be held by you, to value you and be valued by you. With you I will share my joy and my sorrow, my affirmation and my fears, my successes and my failures. I commit myself to the continued growth of our relationship, and I celebrate the joys of our togetherness and love.

Then share together a kiss, or some other nonverbal expression of your love and affection for each other.

After that, pray aloud and together the following prayer:

> God, we know and experience you as love, and in your love we pray that you will affirm and bless our marriage. Help us to develop the openness and honesty, the strength and sharing, the love and vulnerability that will enable us to continue to build a beautiful relationship together. In you, in each other, and in ourselves, may we grow a trusting confidence and faith that will enable us to deal with whatever the future brings. Help us to love, honor and respect each other, and to be the best of friends. May we live so close to each other and to you, and be so responsive to each other's wants and needs, that our life together will be characterized by real peace and love, by deep care and happiness, by joy and fulfillment, and by struggling creatively with our anger and our conflicts and differences. In the growth and development of the coming years, may the commitments of today remain a source of continuing and deepening joy and affection for us, through Jesus Christ, our Lord of Life and Love. Amen.

When you have completed this part of the Service of Commitment, please return to the total group and sit quietly until the other couples have returned.

In the total group, the leader will read the following paraphrase of Paul's words on love from the New Testament, with the hope that these words will reflect and represent what we give to each other and share with each other:

> I will give to you a love that is patient, a love that is kind, a love that endures. I will pledge to you a love that is not jealous or possessive, a love that is not proud

or selfish, a love that is not rude or inconsiderate. My love for you will not insist on its own way, will not be irritable or resentful, will not keep account of wrongs or failures. It will rejoice when good prevails. Our love will know no limit to its endurance, no end to its trust, no fading of its hope. It will outlast everything. Our love will stand when all else around us has fallen. Our life together will have three great qualities: faith . . . hope . . . love, but the greatest of these will be our love for each other.

Each individual will then have the opportunity to verbally complete the following Statement of Affirmation:

"One thing I'd like to affirm about my relationship with (partner's name) is . . . ."

Participation is purely voluntary, and some couples or individuals may choose not to express themselves in this way, at this time.

When those who want to make their Statement of Affirmation have done so, the total group verbally prays together the following prayer:

Be with us God, in our joy and our sorrow, in our love and our anger, in our creativity and our conflict, in our individual lives and in our life as a couple. Be with us in Jesus Christ, in the joy of His spirit, and in the breaking of this loaf and the sharing of this cup. Amen.

The loaf will then be passed and each person will take a piece and hold it, as the leader says, "This is my body which is given for you." The cup will then be passed and one partner dips his piece into the cup, and feeds the other. The cup is then passed to the other partner, who repeats the process. The cup is then passed to the next couple, until all have communed. The words, "This cup is the New Covenant in my blood which is poured out for you for the forgiveness of sins," will be said only once, before the cup is passed to the first couple.

After all have communed, the leader will read "On Love" and "On Marriage" from Kahlil Gibran's *The Prophet.*

The total group will then rise and form a circle and share a group hug, making eye contact with each other and being aware of their feelings toward each other. The group will then break and participate in the Evaluation and Closure experience.

Appendix D

Additional Resources on Marriage Enrichment

In addition to the books describing the specific marriage enrichment programs mentioned in the text, there is an increasing number of books available which may be of value to professionals, leaders of marriage enrichment programs, or couples interested in enhancing their relationships. The sheer number gives some indication of the increasing lay and professional population for which many of these books are written. These books strongly emphasize the need for continual marital and relationship growth, and the need to develop effective interpersonal skills, so that the relationship can be fulfilling and emotionally satisfying to both partners and remain open to effective and creative change. Some are of the textbook type, designed for use in courses on marriage (e.g., Kieren, Henton, and Marotz, 1975; McCary, 1975). The vast majority, however, are oriented towards the general public, and provide couples with detailed instructions for experiences or exercises they can use individually, as a couple, or with other couples, to enhance their relationship (Allred, 1974; Calden, 1975; Clinebell, 1973; Clinebell and Clinebell, 1970; Gottman et al., 1976; Hauck and Kean, 1975; Hunt and Rydman, 1976; Keyes, 1975; Knox, 1975; Mace, 1972; Mace and Mace, 1977; Miller, Nunnally, and Wackman, 1975; Otto, 1969; Powell, 1974; Satir, 1972; Smith and Phillips, 1971; Wackman, Miller, and Nunnally, 1976b; Wilke, 1973). A few of the books (e.g., Lasswell and Lobsenz, 1976) attempt to bridge marriage enrichment and marriage counseling. They express the idea of self-counseling and are aimed at helping couples in the areas of conflict and stress. The authors employ an approach based on the assumption that motivated and committed couples can tap their potential and can learn new skills which will help them make decisions, resolve conflicts, and more effectively meet each other's needs, wants, and expectations.

Only a few of the books dealing with marriage enrichment are written primarily for the professional reader, program facilitator, or leader (e.g., Clinebell, 1975, 1977; Guerney, 1977; L'Abate, 1977a; L'Abate and Collaborators, 1975; Otto, 1976; Smith and Alexander, 1974; Wackman et al., 1976a), and we can only hope that the numbers will increase. Several of those which have appeared to date are written for the professional counselor or therapist (e.g., Clinebell, 1975, 1977; Gottman et al., 1976; Guerney, 1977; Smith and Alexander, 1974).

In addition to these books, several cassette tapes have appeared, designed to guide the professional user in the development of a marriage enrichment program (Clinebell, 1973; Leville, 1972; Malone, 1971, professional version), to guide a couple or group of couples interested in starting a marriage enrichment group (Mace and Mace, 1974a), or to provide a marriage enrichment program for individual couples to use by themselves (Malone, 1971, couple's version). Clinebell (1976) has described the variety of uses to which these cassettes can be applied, and he suggests that cassettes may be particularly useful because of their capacity to augment other live training, and their availability to groups of people who do not have access to other training. Clinebell (1976) and Guerney (1977), as well as others, have incorporated cassette programs into their enrichment process. However, to date, the authors know of no research which demonstrates that the use of a cassette program by itself will lead to substantial improvement in marital adjustment or verbal communication patterns (Williams, 1975).

Notes

1. Mace, D. R. *Preventive training for creative family relationships: Some experiential programs in North America.* Unpublished manuscript, 1978. (Available from Dr. David R. Mace, P.O. Box 5182; Winston-Salem, North Carolina, 27103).
2. L'Abate, L. *Enrichment as prevention: Some possibilities.* Paper presented at the Family Therapy Conference on the Roots of Mental Health, Urban Life Center, Georgia State University, Atlanta, January, 1978.
3. Huber, J. W. *Measuring the effects of Marriage Encounter experience with the caring relationship inventory.* Manuscript submitted for publication, 1977.
4. Hof, L. *Guidelines for referring couples to our Marriage Enrichment program (M.E.P.).* Intra-agency memorandum, Marriage Council of Philadelphia, Inc., 1978.
5. Mace, D. R. Personal communication, March 22, 1978.
6. Witkin, S. *Communication training for couples: A comparative study.* Paper presented at the meeting of the Association for the Advancement of Behavior Therapy, Atlanta, December, 1977.

References

Alexander J: Defensive and supportive communication in normal and deviant families. *J Consult Clin Psychol, 40,* 223-231, 1973

Allred GH: *How to strengthen your marriage and family.* Provo, Utah: Brigham Young Press, 1974

Bach G, and Wyden P: *The intimate enemy.* New York: William Morrow, 1969

Balswick JO, and Peck CW: The unexpressive male: An American tragedy. *The Family Coordinator, 20,* 363-368, 1971

Beaver WA: *Conjoint and pseudo-disjunctive treatment in communication skills for relationship improvement with marital couples.* Unpublished doctoral dissertation, Marquette University, 1978

Beck DF: Research findings on the outcome of marital counseling. *Social Casework, 56,* 153-181, 1975

Bednar RL, Melnick J, and Kaul J: Risk, responsibility, and structure: A conceptual framework for initiating group counseling and psychotherapy. *J Couns Psycho, 24,* 31-37, 1974

Berman EM, and Lief HI: Marital therapy from a psychiatric perspective: An overview. *Am J Psychiatry, 132,* 583-592, 1975

Berne E: *Games people play.* New York: Grove, 1964

Berne E: *Principles of group treatment.* New York: Grove, 1968

Bolte GL: A communication approach to marital counseling. *In AS Gurman & DG Rice, Eds., Couples in conflict.* New York: Jason Aronson, 1975

Bosco A: *Marriage Encounter, a rediscovery of love.* St. Meinrad, Ind.: Abbey, 1973

Brown R: *The effects of couple communication training on traditional sex stereotypes of husbands and wives.* Unpublished master's thesis, Appalachian State University, 1976

Bruder AH: *Effects of a marriage enrichment program upon marital communication and adjustment.* Unpublished doctoral dissertation, Purdue University, 1972

Buckland CM: An educational model of family consultation. *J Marr Fam Couns, 3*(3), 49-56, 1977

Burns CW: *Effectiveness of the basic encounter group in marriage counseling.* Unpublished doctoral dissertation, University of Oklahoma, 1972

Calden G: *I count—You count: The "do it ourselves" marriage counseling and enrichment book.* Niles, Ill.: Argus, 1975

Campbell EE: *The effects of couple communication training on married couples in the child-rearing years.* Unpublished doctoral dissertation, Arizona State University, 1974

Clarke C: Group procedures for increasing positive feedback between married partners. *The Family Coordinator, 19,* 324-328, 1970

Clinebell CH: *Meet me in the middle.* New York: Harper & Row, 1973

Clinebell HJ: *Growth counseling. Part 1: Enriching marriage and family life.* (Cassette tape) Nashville: Abingdon, 1973

Clinebell HJ: *Growth counseling for marriage enrichment.* Philadelphia: Fortress, 1975

Clinebell HJ: Cassette programs for training and enrichment. *In* HA Otto, Ed., *Marriage and family enrichment: New perspectives and programs.* Nashville: Abingdon, 1976

Clinebell HJ: *Growth counseling for mid-years couples.* Philadelphia: Fortress, 1977

Clinebell HJ, and Clinebell CH: *The intimate marriage.* New York: Harper & Row, 1970

Collins JD: *The effects of the Conjugal Relationship modification method on marital communication and adjustment.* Unpublished doctoral dissertation, Pennsylvania State University, 1971

Collins JD: Experimental evaluation of a six-month conjugal therapy and relationship enhancement program. *In* BG Guerney, Jr., *Relationship Enhancement.* San Francisco: Jossey-Bass, 1977

Cozby PW: Self disclosure: A literative review. *Psychological Bulletin, 79,* 73–91, 1973

D'Augelli AR, Deyss DS, Guerney BG, Jr., et al.: Interpersonal skill training for dating couples: An evaluation of an educational mental health service. *J Couns Psychol, 21,* 385–389, 1974

Demarest D, Sexton J, and Sexton M: *Marriage Encounter.* St. Paul: Carillon, 1977

Derlega V, and Chaikin A: *Sharing intimacy: What we reveal to others and why.* Englewood Cliffs, NJ: Prentice-Hall, 1975

DeRosis HA: Parent group discussions: A preventive mental health technique. *The Family Coordinator, 19,* 329–334, 1970

Dillon J: *Marital communication and its relation to self-esteem.* Unpublished doctoral dissertation, United States International University, 1975

Dixon DN, and Sciara AD: Effectiveness of group reciprocity counseling with married couples. *J Marr Fam Couns, 3*(3), 77–83, 1977

Doherty WJ, McCabe P, and Ryder RG: Marriage Encounter: A critical appraisal. *J Marr Fam Couns, 4,* 99–107, 1978

Egan G: *Encounter: Group process for interpersonal growth.* Belmont, Ca.: Brooks/Cole, 1970

Eisenberg L: Possibilities for a preventive psychiatry. *Pediatrics, 30,* 815–828, 1962

Ellis A: Techniques of handling anger in marriage. *J Marr Fam Couns, 2,* 305–315, 1976

Ely AL, Guerney BG, Jr., and Stover L: Efficacy of the training phase of conjugal therapy. *Psychotherapy: Theory, research and practice, 10,* 201–207, 1973

Epstein N, and Jackson E: An outcome study of short-term communication training with married couples. *J Consult Clin Psychol, 46,* 207–212, 1978

Fisher RE: *The effect of two group counseling methods on perceptual congruence in married pairs.* Unpublished doctoral dissertation, University of Hawaii, 1973

Foote NN: Matching of husband and wife in phases of development. *In* MB Sussman, Ed., *Sourcebook of marriage and the family.* Boston: Houghton Mifflin, 1963

Gallagher C: *The Marriage Encounter: As I have loved you.* Garden City, NY: Doubleday, 1975

Genovese RJ: Marriage Encounter. *Small Group Behavior, 6,* 45–56, 1975

Gilbert SJ: Self disclosure, intimacy and communication in families. *The Family Coordinator, 25,* 221–231, 1976

Gilbert SJ, and Horenstein D: A study of self-disclosure: Level vs. valence. *J Hum Comm Research,* Fall, 1975

Ginsberg B, and Vogelsong E: Premarital relationship improvement by maximizing empathy and self-disclosure. *In* BG Guerney, *Relationship enhancement,* San Francisco: Jossey-Bass, 1977

Glasser LN, and Glasser PH: Hedonism and the family: Conflict in values? *J Marr Fam Couns, 3*(4), 11–18, 1977

Goldstein AP: Domains and dilemmas. *Int J Psychiatry, 7,* 128–134, 1969

Goldstein AP: *Structured learning therapy.* New York: Academic Press, 1973

Goldstein AP, Heller K, and Sechrest LB: *Psychotherapy and the psychology of behavior change.* New York: John Wiley and Sons, 1966

Gordon T: *Parent Effectiveness Training.* New York: Wyden, 1970

Gottman J, Notarius C, Gonso J, and Markman H: *A couple's guide to communication.* Champaign, Ill.: Research Press, 1976

Guerney BG, Jr: *Psychotherapeutic agents: New roles for nonprofessionals, parents, and teachers.* New York: Holt, Rinehart & Winston, 1969

Guerney BG, Jr: *Relationship Enhancement.* San Francisco: Jossey-Bass, 1977

Guerney BG, Jr: Evaluation of consultation—Supervision in training conjugal therapists. *Professional Psychology, 9,* 203–209, 1978

Guldner CA: Family therapy for the trainee in family therapy. *J Marr Fam Couns, 4*(1), 127–132, 1978

Gurman AS, and Kniskern SP: Enriching research on marital enrichment programs. *J Marr Fam Couns, 3*(2), 3–11, 1977

Harrell J, and Guerney BG, Jr: Training married couples in conflict negotiation skills. *In* DHL Olson, Ed., *Treating relationships.* Lake Mills, Iowa: Graphic, 1976

Hauck P, and Kean ES: *Marriage and the memo method.* Philadelphia: Westminster, 1975

Hines GA: Efficacy of communication skills training with married partners where no marital counseling has been sought (Doctoral dissertation, University of South Dakota, 1975). *Dissertation Abstracts International, 36,* 5045–5046A, 1976

Hopkins L, and Hopkins P: Marriage enrichment and the churches. *Spectrum,* Fall, 1975

Hopkins L, Hopkins P, Mace D, and Mace V: *Toward better marriages.* Winston-Salem: ACME, 1978

Horney K: *Our inner conflicts.* New York: Norton, 1945

Horowitz M: On the cognitive structure of interpersonal problems treated in psychotherapy. *Consult Clin Psycho, 47,* 5–15, 1979

Hunt RA, and Rydman EJ: *Creative Marriage.* Boston: Holbrook, 1976

Hurvitz N: *Marital roles inventory manual.* Beverly Hills: Western Psychological Services, 1961

Jacobson NS, and Martin B: Behavioral marriage therapy: Current status. *Psychological Bulletin, 83,* 540–556, 1976

James M, and Jongeward D: *Born to win.* Reading, Mass.: Addison-Wesley, 1971

Jourard SM: *The transparent self.* New York: Van Nostrand, 1964

Jourard SM: *Self disclosure.* New York: Van Nostrand, 1971

Jourard, SM and Richman P: Factors in the self-disclosure input of college students. *Merrill-Palmer Quarterly, 9,* 141–148, 1963

Kagan J, and Kogan N: Individual variation in cognitive processes. *In* PH Mussan, Ed., *Carmichael's manual of child psychology,* Vol. 1. New York: Wiley, 1970

Keyes M: *Staying married.* Millbrae, Ca.: Les Femmes, 1975

Kieren D, Henton J, and Marotz R: *His and hers: A problem solving approach to marriage.* Hinsdale, Ill.: Dryden, 1975

Kilmann PR, Julian A, and Moreault D: The impact of a marriage enrichment program on relationship factors. *J Sex Marital Ther, 4,* 298–303, 1978

Kilmann PR, Moreault D, and Robinson EA: Effects of a marriage enrichment program: An outcome study. *J Sex Marital Ther, 4,* 54–57, 1978

Knox D: *Dr. Knox's marital exercise book.* New York: McKay, 1975

Koch T, and Koch L: Marriage enrichment courses: The urgent drive to make good marriages better. *Psychology Today,* September *10,* 33–35; 83; 85; 95, 1976

Kolb DA: Disciplinary inquiry norms and student learning styles: Diverse pathways for growth. In A Chickering Ed., *The future American college.* San Francisco: Jossey-Bass, 1979

Kurtz RR: Structured experiences in groups: A theoretical and research discussion. *In* JW Pfeiffer and JE Jones, Eds., *The 1975 annual handbook for group facilitators.* La Jolla, Ca.: University Associates, 1975

L'Abate L: Family enrichment programs. _J Fam Couns, 2_(1), 32–38, 1974

L'Abate L: _Enrichment: Structured interventions with couples, families, and groups._ Washington, DC: University Press of America, 1977

L'Abate L: Intimacy is sharing hurt feelings: A reply to David Mace. _J Marr Fam Couns, 3_(2), 13–16, 1977

L'Abate L, and Collaborators: _Manual: Enrichment programs for the family life cycle._ Atlanta: Social Research Laboratories, 1975

L'Abate L, and Weeks G: Testing the limits of enrichment: When enrichment is not enough. _J Fam Couns, 4_(1), 70–74, 1976

Larsen GR: An evaluation of the Minnesota Couples Communication Program's influence on marital communication and self and mate perceptions (Doctoral dissertation, Arizona State University, 1974). _Dissertation Abstracts International, 35,_ 2625–2628A, 1974

Lasswell M, and Lobsenz N: _No-fault marriage: The new technique of self-counseling and what it can help you do._ Garden City: Doubleday, 1976

Lederer WJ, and Jackson DD: _The mirages of marriage._ New York: Norton, 1968

Leville GT: _Making marriage work._ New York: Paulist Press, (Cassette tape) 1972

Levinson DJ: _The seasons of a man's life._ New York: Afred A. Knopf, 1978

Liberman RP, Wheeler E, and Sanders N: Behavioral therapy for marital disharmony. _J Marr Fam Couns, 2,_ 383–395, 1976

Lieberman MA, Yalom ID and Miles MB: _Encounter groups: First facts._ New York: Basic Books, 1973

Lief HI: Sensitivity to feelings. _J Am Acad Psychoanal, 5,_ 289–290, 1977

Lo Piccolo J, and Miller V: A program for enhancing the sexual relationship of normal couples. _In_ J and L Lo Piccolo, Ed., _Handbook of sex therapy._ New York: Plenum Press, 1978

Luft J: _Of human interaction._ Palo Alto: Mayfield, 1969

Luthman SG, and Kirschenbaum M: _The dynamic family._ Palo Alto: Science and Behavior, 1974

Mace DR: _Getting ready for marriage._ Nashville: Abingdon, 1972

Mace DR: Marriage enrichment concepts for research. _The Family Coordinator, 24,_ 171–173, (a) 1975

Mace DR: We call it ACME. _Small Group Behavior, 6,_ 31–44, (b) 1975

Mace DR: Marital intimacy and the deadly love-anger cycle. _J Marr Fam Couns, 2,_ 131–137, 1976

Mace D, and Mace V: _Introducing ACME_ and _How to start a marriage enrichment group._ Winston-Salem: ACME, (a) (Cassette tape) 1974

Mace D, and Mace V: _We can have better marriages if we really want them._ Nashville: Abingdon, (b) 1974

Mace D, and Mace V: Marriage enrichment—Wave of the future? _The Family Coordinator, 24,_ 131–135, 1975

Mace D, and Mace V: _Marriage enrichment—A preventive group approach for couples. In_ DHL Olson Ed., _Treating relationships._ Lake Mills, Iowa: Graphic, (a) 1976

Mace D, and Mace V: The selection, training and certification of facilitators for marriage enrichment programs. _The Family Coordinator, 25,_ 117–125, (b) 1976

Mace D, and Mace V: _How to have a happy marriage._ Nashville: Abingdon, 1977

Mace D, and Mace V: The marriage enrichment movement: Its history, its rationale, and its future prospects. _In_ L and P Hopkins and D and V Mace, _Toward better marriages._ Winston-Salem: ACME, 1978

Maddock JW: Sexual health: An enrichment and treatment program. _In_ DHL Olson, Ed., _Treating relationships._ Lake Mills, Iowa: Graphic, 1976

Malamud DI: Communication training in the second chance family. _In_ S Miller, Ed., _Marriages and families: Enrichment through communication._ Beverly Hills: Sage, 1975

Malone TP: _Marriage enrichment program._ Chicago: Human Development Institute, (Cassette tape) 1971

McCary JL: _Freedom and growth in marriage._ Santa Barbara: Hamilton, 1975

McIntosh DM: A comparison of the effects of highly structured, partially structured, and non-structured human relations training for married couples on the dependent variables of communication, marital adjustment, and personal adjustment (Doctoral dissertation, North Texas State University, 1975). *Dissertation Abstracts International, 36,* 2636-2637A, 1975

McLeish J, Matheson W, and Park J: *Psychology of the learning group.* London: Hutchinson, 1973

Miller S: *The effects of communication training in small groups upon self-disclosure and openness in engaged couples' systems of interaction: A field experiment.* Unpublished doctoral dissertation, University of Minnesota, 1971

Miller S, Ed.: *Marriages and families: Enrichment through communication.* Beverly Hills: Sage, 1975

Miller S, Corrales R, and Wackman DB: Recent progress in understanding and facilitating marital communication. *The Family Coordinator, 24,* 143-152, 1975

Miller S, Nunnally E, and Wackman DB: *Alive and aware.* Minneapolis: Interpersonal Communications Programs, 1975

Miller S, Nunnally EW, and Wackman DB: A communication training program for couples. *Social Casework, 57,* 9-18, (a) 1976

Miller S, Nunnally EW, and Wackman DB: Minnesota Couples Communication Program (MCCP): Premarital and marital groups. In DHL Olson, Ed., *Treating relationships.* Lake Mills, Iowa: Graphic, (b) 1976

Nadeau KG: *An examination of some effects of the marital enrichment group.* Unpublished doctoral dissertation, University of Florida, 1971

Navran L: Communication and adjustment in marriage. *Family Process, 6,* 173-184, 1967

Neville WG: An analysis of personality types and their differential response to marital enrichment groups (Doctoral dissertation, University of Florida, 1971). *Dissertation Abstracts International, 32*(12-A), 6766, 1971

Nunnally EW: *Effects of communication training upon interaction awareness and empathic accuracy of engaged couples: A field experiment.* Unpublished doctoral dissertation, University of Minnesota, 1971

Nunnally EW, Miller S, and Wackman DB. The Minnesota Couples Communication Program. *Small Group Behavior, 6,* 57-71, 1975

Olson DHL: *Treating relationships.* Lake Mills, Iowa: Graphic, 1976

Orling RA: The efficacy of proactive marital communication training (Doctoral dissertation, New Mexico State University, 1974). *Dissertation Abstracts International, 36,* 3618-3619B, 1976

Otto HA: *More joy in your marriage.* New York: Hawthorne, 1969

Otto HA: *The utilization of family strengths in marriage and family counseling.* Beverly Hills: Holistic, 1972

Otto HA: Marriage and family enrichment programs in North America—Report and analysis. *The Family Coordinator, 24,* 137-142, 1975

Otto HA, Ed.: *Marriage and family enrichment: New perspectives and programs.* Nashville: Abingdon, 1976

Paul N, and Paul B: *A marital puzzle.* New York: Norton, 1975

Phillips EL, and Wiener DN: *Short-term psychotherapy and structured behavioral change.* New York: McGraw-Hill, 1966

Piaget J: *The place of the sciences of man in the system of sciences.* New York: Harper Torchbooks, 1970

Pilder SJ: *Some effects of laboratory training on married couples.* Unpublished doctoral dissertation, United States International University, 1972

Powell J: *The secret of staying in love.* Niles, Ill.: Argus, 1974

Rappaport, AF: Conjugal Relationship Enhancement Program. *In* DHL Olson, Ed., *Treating relationships.* Lake Mills, Iowa: Graphic, 1976

Rappaport AF, and Harrell JE: A behavioral exchange model for marital counseling. *In* AS Gurman and DG Rice, Eds., *Couples in conflict.* New York: Jason Aronson, 1975

Regula RB: Marriage Encounter: What makes it work? *The Family Coordinator, 24,* 153–159, 1975

Roberts PV: The effects on marital satisfaction of brief training in behavioral exchange negotiation mediated by differentially experienced trainers (Doctoral dissertation, Fuller Theological Seminary, 1974). *Dissertation Abstracts International, 36,* 457B, 1975

Rogers CR: *Becoming partners: Marriage and its alternatives.* New York: Delacorte, 1972

Roszak B, and Roszak T, Eds.: *Masculine/feminine: Readings in sexual mythology and the liberation of women.* New York: Harper & Row, 1969

Satir VM: Conjoint marital therapy. *In* BL Green, Ed., *The psychotherapies of marital disharmony.* New York: Free Press, 1965

Satir VM: *Conjoint family therapy.* Palo Alto: Science & Behavior, 1967

Satir VM: *Peoplemaking.* Palo Alto: Science & Behavior, 1972

Sauber, SR: Primary prevention and the marital enrichment group. *J Fam Couns, 2*(1), 39–44, 1974

Schauble PG, and Hill CG: A laboratory approach to treatment in marriage counseling: Training in communication skills. *The Family Coordinator, 25,* 277–284, 1976

Schlien SR: *Training dating couples in empathic and open communication: An experimental evaluation of a potential preventative mental health program.* Unpublished doctoral dissertation, Pennsylvania State University, 1971

Schutz WC: *FIRO (the interpersonal underworld).* Palo Alto: Science and Behavior, 1966

Schutz WC: *Here comes everybody.* New York: Harper & Row, 1971

Schutz WC: Encounter. *In* R Corsini, Ed., *Current psychotherapies.* Itasca, Ill.: Peacock, 1973

Schutz WC: *FIRO awareness scales manual.* Palo Alto: Consulting Psychologists Press, 1978

Schwager HA, and Conrad RW: *Impact of group counseling on self and other acceptance and persistence with rural disadvantaged student families* (Counseling Services Report No. 15). Washington, DC: National Institute of Education, 1974

Sheehy G: *Passages.* New York: E.P. Dutton, 1974

Shelton JL, and Ackerman JM: *Homework in counseling and psychotherapy.* Springfield, Ill.: Thomas, 1974

Sherwood JJ, and Glidewell JC: Planned renegotiation: A norm-setting OD intervention. *In* JW Pfieffer and JE Jones, Eds., *The 1973 annual handbook for group facilitators.* La Jolla, CA: University Associates, 1973

Sherwood JJ, and Scherer JJ: A model for couples: How two can grow together. *In* S Miller, Ed., *Marriages and families: Enrichment through communication.* Beverly Hills, Sage, 1975

Shostrom EL: *Caring Relationship Inventory.* San Diego: EDITS/Educational and Industrial Testing Service, 1967

Skinner BF: *Science and human behavior.* New York: Macmillan, 1953

Skinner BF: *Contingencies of reinforcement.* New York: Appleton-Century-Crofts, 1969

Smith G, and Phillips AI: *Me and you and us.* New York: Wyden, 1971

Smith L, and Smith A: Developing a national marriage communication lab training program. *In* HA Otto, Ed., *Marriage and family enrichment: New perspectives and programs.* Nashville: Abingdon, 1976

Smith RL, and Alexander AM: *Counseling couples in groups.* Springfield, Ill: Thomas, 1974

Stein EV: MARDILAB: An experiment in marriage enrichment. *The Family Coordinator, 24,* 167–170, 1975

Swicegood ML: *An evaluative study of one approach to marriage enrichment.* Unpublished doctoral dissertation, University of North Carolina at Greensboro, 1974

Thielen A, Hubner HO, and Schmook C: *Studies of the effectiveness of the German revised version of the Minnesota Couples Communication Program on relationships between partners.* Institute of Psychology, University of Heidelberg, 1976

Travis RP, and Travis PY: The Pairing Enrichment Program: Actualizing the marriage. *The Family Coordinator, 24,* 161–165, 1975

Travis RP, and Travis PY: Self-actualization in marital enrichment. *J Marr Fam Couns, 2,* 73–80, (a) 1976

Travis RP, and Travis PY: A note on changes in the caring relationship following a marriage enrichment program and some preliminary findings. *J Marr Fam Couns, 2,* 81–83, (b) 1976

Truax CB, and Carkhuff RR: *Toward effective counseling and psychotherapy.* Chicago: Aldine, 1967

Van Zoost B: Premarital communication skills education with university couples. *The Family Coordinator, 22,* 187–191, 1973

Venema HB: Marriage enrichment: A comparison of the behavior exchange negotiation and communication models (Doctoral dissertation, Fuller Theological Seminary, 1975). *Dissertation Abstracts International, 36,* 4184–4185B, 1976

Vincent CE: *Sexual and marital health.* New York: McGraw-Hill, 1973

Vincent CE: Barriers to the development of marital health as a health field. *J Marr Fam Couns, 3*(3), 3–11, 1977

Wackman DB, Miller S, and Nunnally EW: *Alive and aware: Improving communications in relationships—Classroom instructor manual.* Minneapolis: Interpersonal Communication Programs, (a) 1976

Wackman DB, Miller S, and Nunnally EW: *Student workbook: Increasing awareness and communication skills.* Minneapolis: Interpersonal Communication Programs, (b) 1976

Watzlawick P, Beavin J, and Jackson D: *Pragmatics of human communication.* New York: Norton, 1967

Weinstein CG: Differential change in self-actualizing and self-concept, and its effects on marital interaction, as an outcome of a selected growth group experience (Doctoral dissertation, University of Southern California, 1975). *Dissertation Abstracts International, 36,* 4067–4068A, 1975

Widick C, and Cowan M: How developmental theory can assist facilitators to select and design structured experiences. *In* CG Carney and SL McMahon, Eds., *Exploring contemporary male/female roles: A facilitator's guide.* La Jolla, CA: University Associates, 1977

Wieman RJ: *Conjugal relationship modification and reciprocal reinforcement: A comparison of treatments for marital discord.* Unpublished doctoral dissertation, Pennsylvania State University, 1973

Wilke RB: *Tell me again, I'm listening.* Nashville: Abingdon, 1973

Williams AM: *Comparison of the effects of two marital enrichment programs on marital communication and adjustment.* Unpublished master's thesis, University of Florida, 1975

Wright L, and L'Abate L: Four approaches to family facilitation. *The Family Coordinator, 26,* 176–181, 1977

Yalom ID: *The theory and practice of group psychotherapy.* New York: Basic Books, 1970

Zinker JC, and Leon JP: The Gestalt perspective: A marriage enrichment program. *In* HA Otto Ed., *Marriage and family enrichment: New perspectives and programs.* Nashville: Abingdon, 1976

Credits

Grateful acknowledgment is given to the authors and publishers
for permission to use the following material:

Chapter 1

The quotation from Karen Horney, *Our Inner Conflicts,* 1945, is printed here by permission of the publisher, W.W. Norton Co., Inc.

Chapter 2

The criteria for appropriate self-disclosure are from *Of Human Interaction,* 1969, by Joseph Luft, and are printed here by permission of the publisher, Mayfield Publishing Co.

The list of curative factors in group therapy is from I.D. Yalom, *The Theory and Practice of Group Psychotherapy,* 1970, and is used here by permission of the publisher, Basic Books, Inc.

The discussion of the theoretical foundation of marriage enrichment programming is greatly influenced by B.G. Guerney, *Relationship Enhancement,* 1977. The ideas referring to Rogerian psychotherapy and behavior modification therapy are used by permission of the publisher, Jossey-Bass, Inc.

Chapter 1 and 3

The purposes of ACME listed in Chapter 1, the training and certification standards, and the marriage enrichment program guidelines listed in Chapter 3 are from the Handbook of the Association of Couples for Marriage Enrichment (ACME), *Toward Better Marriages* (1978), by L. and P. Hopkins, and D. and V. Mace, and are used here by permission of ACME.

Chapter 6

Some of the material describing William Schutz's concepts of Inclusion, Control and Affection is quoted or paraphrased from William Schutz, "Encounter," *In* R. Corsini, Editor, *Current Psychotherapies,* 1973, and is used by permission of the publisher, F.E. Peacock Publishers, Inc.

The definitions of Inclusion, Control, and Affection are from the FIRO Awareness Scales Manual, 1978, by William Schutz, and are printed here by permission of the publisher, Consulting Psychologists Press.

Chapter 7

The Individual and Marriage Strengths Listing exercise is adapted from Herbert A. Otto's Sharing Marriage Strengths, and His Strengths-Her Strengths exercises, in *More Joy in Your Marriage,* 1969, by permission of the author.